Sail the World?

An Absurdly True Story

Prequel to *RV the World*

By

David Rich

ISBN 978-1-7379279-0-7

Maps courtesy of openstreetmap.com. Photos by David Rich. This is an absurdly true story direct from the annals of the author's journal, with the name of only a single character changed to protect the less than innocent

Direct inquiries to *David Rich* at jdavidrich@yahoo.com

ALSO BY DAVID RICH

RV the World, 2nd Edition

Myths of the Tribe - When Religion and Ethics Diverge

Scribes of the Tribe - The Great Thinkers on Religion and Ethics

The ISIS Affair - Putting the Fun Back in Fundamentalism

Antelopes - A Modern Gulliver's Travels

Sail the World? is dedicated to my Honey Bunny Mary Alexon, and to our good friend who accompanied us on numerous sailing charters, Morgan Riley (RIP 2020)

Contents

1

May-June 1993

My thirty-five-foot Erickson sailboat was sinking in the Pacific Ocean. I'd bragged about sailing around the world but two hours after leaving Todos Santos Sur, an island a few miles off Ensenada, Mexico, I was slip-sliding around searching for the source of a colossal leak, enveloped in an eerie blanket of fog with zero visibility and surrounded by invisible hazards. Glub, glub. The floorboards were floating as I ran below, stubbing fingers, frantically yanking open cupboard doors, looking for ruptured water lines. If my longtime girlfriend Mary had come along as planned, I wouldn't be in this predicament. Solo sailing seriously sucked.

I feverishly searched the lockers on the starboard side, flipping red levers to close through-valves, unable to find the leak that threatened to destroy years of planning and everything I owned. A life jacket bobbed in the galley as I yanked open another locker. No leak there either.

Whirling dervishes had nothing on me. I was all over the boat, pulling everything out of lockers, checking nine through-hulls. I found no leaks, but the second I stopped holding down the manual switch for the bilge pump, the bilge began refilling. I couldn't tell where the water was coming from. I must have been insane, sailing a small vessel single-handedly on the largest ocean in the world.

Erickson had manufactured the boat I named *Grendel* long before General Motors built the first fiberglass car and the Corvette made fiberglass a thing. *Grendel* was ancient, closer to the Clipper Era when half the crew died while rounding the Horn. By the 1990s, fiberglass boats were made paper-thin, but *Grendel* was an inch thick, a comfort off lee shores and among whales butting boats. Whale collisions sank more boats than any other known cause, but then most causes were unknown, such as in the Bermuda Triangle. Here in Mexico, boats usually sank because of severe weather or collisions with shrimp boats running without lights. Two shrimpers had almost rammed me, materializing out of the dense fog, missing me by inches, but that wasn't why *Grendel* was sinking.

The cause was my stupidity, but that will have to wait until the next chapter because I first need to explain how I blundered into this mess--on land and at sea.

Friends said I was crazy. "But you live in Arizona. There's no water, except a few ridiculous lakes." Or, "How bizarre, a guy from ocean-less Arizona, retiring early to sail around the world in a little old sailboat..." Ignoring the ribbing, I resigned from an ultra-cushy job as an assistant attorney general supervising lawyers overseeing the legal affairs of most state agencies in Arizona, ranging from the prison system to the courts and the unsupervisable legislature. I managed early retirement a few weeks before my fiftieth birthday and sold everything that wouldn't fit on a sailboat: house, car, and bulky belongings.

I thought I was ready because I'd sailed all over the world, through storms from the Bermuda Triangle to the vicious Meltemi winds in the Greek Islands. I'd also taken two captains' courses, read all the classic books on sailing, and captained seventeen charters from Belize to Turkey and all over the Caribbean. But I was flat-out wrong.

I wasn't the mechanical type, which made this adventure straight out of *Dragnet* on old-time radio: *dumb da dumb dumb.* Flunking grade school shop should have tipped me off right away. I was a passable sailor but had to rely on boatyards and friends to install, repair, and maintain most of the equipment on the boat.

My girlfriend Mary and I had spent years outfitting *Grendel,* moored in San Diego Harbor across from the airport. This was convenient from Phoenix, only twenty-nine dollars on Southwest Airlines. We flew over on weekends, spending several years adding many of the goodies needed for ocean sailing, from mast steps to a watermaker that made seawater drinkable.

Grendel with Dave and Mary aboard

Four months before I left, Mary decided she couldn't go because, at age forty-three, she didn't think she'd saved up enough money to retire. I was devastated and depressed because this broke up the relationship after we'd spent almost ten years saving every penny to realize our dream of sailing around the world together.

Retiring early to travel had always been my goal, beginning with childhood memories of a geography book stuffed with full-color prints of Vesuvius erupting and frying rich Romans in Pompei, and Mary loved to travel. The dream of world-travel sustained me through government bureaucracy, faculty intrigue while teaching at the local law school, dealing with litigants as a *pro tem* judge and with hapless clients in private practice. I couldn't and wouldn't give up the dream, even for Mary, though she was the best and most seductive relationship I'd ever had.

We were also among the most independent and headstrong individuals on the planet. During the two years after we met, Mary and I dumped each other twice while gradually escaping from entanglements with others. The second time I dumped her, we hugged goodbye in the parking lot of our favorite restaurant in Phoenix, inadvertently revealing the basis for a fatal attraction about which I've been advised to say nothing further. The attraction was sealed a few months later when we moved in together, lasting seven years until she decided against retiring early. I could only press onward.

I knew San Diego was way too expensive for final preparations, so I sailed down to the Ensenada boatyard in Mexico, sixty miles south of San Diego. With hourly rates a fourth of that in San Diego, Ensenada was a better option for installing final touches. I liked Ensenada, but I loved to travel anywhere and everywhere. Destinations were unimportant.

Ensenada

Grendel sat on the hard at the Baja Naval boatyard in Ensenada. Luckily, my favorite entertainment was right next door at LF Caliente, a sports bar and betting emporium. Before retiring, I owned Phoenix Suns season tickets for twenty-one years, sitting in front of the owner, Jerry Colangelo, at games played in a venue I represented as counsel. We'd run into each other on weekends at AJ's fancy grocery emporium and analyze the Suns, mostly to no avail because in all these years, the Suns made the NBA Finals only once, waiting for the second time until I left town. At least I could watch the 1993 NBA Finals featuring Charles Barkley of *my* Phoenix Suns while quaffing Dos Equis *cerveza* in a frosty mug. The waiter had mistaken me for a well-known race car driver—accidentally, of course. This resulted in superb service and he swooped in with a fresh shot glass of limes with every beer. Barkley pirouetted until Jordan tripped him up, then Sir Charles muffed the winning basket, and the Suns dropped their second NBA Finals game. Hey, it was in Chicago. For the next game, we'd have the home-court advantage.

Grendel on the hard in Ensenada

I stepped outside and vendors yelled, "Hey, mister. Fish taco?" Fishmongers repelled swarms of flies with streamers, whisking over a feast of oysters, crab, and clams, protecting my favorite cuisine, seafood of any make or model. I ordered three jumbo shrimp tacos and a strawberry soda, $3.50 and yummy. I'd eaten at street vendors in many countries and loved them because, as opposed to sit-down restaurants, you can watch the food being prepared right in front of you.

I alternated seafood with visits to a favorite fast-food cart pushed by a guy who looked a lot like Steve McQueen in a sombrero. After I'd scarfed down three mini-tacos, *Señor* McQueen took a kilo of gleaming white lard and shimmered it off the sizzling metal dome. It sizzled and glistened in waxy rivulets under the sickly yellow streetlight, flowing into a pool of grease beside mounds of pork and beef. I promptly ordered two more undeniably delicious tacos.

With *Grendel* out of the water, sitting on the hard, I had no way to shower on board or even wash my hands. So, every other day I climbed down a nine-foot ladder from *Grendel*'s deck and walked across town, past the plaza

9

where cruise-ship shuttle-buses dropped *gringos* in massive loads and carriages with pink and black leather seats hitched to fancily decorated horses. I turned through the red-light district, past Candiles Nightclub, Hotel Califia, PARIS, Barloenti Bar, and half a dozen others, ducking into an alley after a long block north, where I opened a door that listed daily hours, 8 a.m. to 9 p.m. I paid a lady twelve pesos, the equivalent of four dollars, and in return received a waistcloth, towel, and a tiny lock and key.

On this most memorable day, I rushed to my assigned cubicle, looking forward to *al vapor* because I'd always loved the steam baths. They were great places to relax, and more importantly for the impecunious in Ensenada, they offered the only hot showers outside of expensive hotel rooms. The was a single drawback. I couldn't wear my glasses, which I'd worn from age five, making me blind and paranoid.

A plastic-covered couch filled the closet-sized dressing room, lit by a hand-tightened bulb that always burned my fingers when I twisted it off. I wrapped the threadbare cloth around my waist and entered a common area that smelled like a swamp, flanked by a steam-room, sauna, and weight room. Men sat on benches or shaved at grungy basins, wearing a third of a worn sheet. A chap who lifted weights or gulped steroids lay on the massage table in the middle of the room, still dripping from a shower.

I dropped my stuff and blindly entered the steam room where pale light peeked through the mist, feeling around to find a space on an almost invisible bench circling the room. As my vision cleared, a hairy guy three feet away grabbed my attention, practicing his long stroke, merrily pulling his pud like a rubber band. I sat frozen, gripped by the ridiculous idea that it wouldn't be polite to jump up and dash from the room. But even out of the corner of my eye, I couldn't ignore the taffy-pulling rhythm, so I pretended to casually stretch, unable to wait a second longer, running out the door in jerky steps, ending my longest thirty seconds in memory. But at least I finally understood the funny look I got from the owner of the boatyard when I told him how much I loved the steam baths.

The boat was filthy, littered with shavings of fiberglass, copper, brass, and teak spread by workmen who'd branded my bunk in the pointy end with footprints, crawling all over it while compartmentalizing two anchoring systems. I'd packed, unpacked, and repacked the lockers while installing cleats, anchors, a V-berth door, and a head. We'd repaired the floor and bilge, and installed the watermaker, a shower pump, radar, an HF radio system, and a propane stove.

I spent five weeks ineptly supervising and organizing my pipe dream, juggling boatyard workers and Marty, my mechanically talented buddy who drove down from Cardiff on the Sea to assist when not toiling at Scripps Institution of Oceanography. Then *Grendel* was almost ready to launch and friends flew to Ensenada for a farewell party. I thought it strange they wanted to celebrate my departure at the nudie shows in the fleshpots of Ensenada, but hey, they were friends so we walked the red-light district on sidewalks unswept since the reign of Maximillian. The garish neon lights painted most of the night ladies as romantic and alluring, though drunks lunged from hidden doorways, sometimes in pairs and with nefarious intent, muted when they spied a *gringo*. Greenbacks were the mainstay of the Ensenada economy and Americans were a protected species. For friend Jerry from Tucson, the evening would frame a story as current as the 1993 Academy Awards. A story he'd forget to tell his grandchildren.

Hooker hangouts masqueraded as disco bars. The classier ones, a half dozen out of twenty, displayed dancers' pictures behind glass, and five of my friends peeled off to watch a show while two breathtaking lovelies stood on the sidewalk, beckoning. Jerry chatted one up while I stood guard, worried about Jerry, an attorney I'd supervised and who spent his vacations in Bangkok. While he negotiated, I fended off drunks and less attractive members of the world's oldest profession.

Jerry picked a Nancy Kwan look-alike with a perfect face, high cheekbones, and fingers like daggers. Her arms were lithe and blouse low-cut, emphasizing maximum headlights over a miniskirt six inches long. She had legs without end, triangulated over spike heels. A knockout, which was another thing I hoped Jerry was worried about.

"Twenty dollars, mister."

Jerry was drooling because she also smelled nice. Especially compared to the looped hooker I retreated from when she attempted a crotch dance on my thigh. No two creatures could present such a contrast. My poor molester wore combat pants, boots, and a silk shirt, tongue flopping as she screamed at the top of her lungs, "Suckee, fuckee." I hated to be touched by strangers, and I retreated from the shrill screeching that no one else seemed to pay the slightest attention to.

Ms. Kwan demurely pulled Jerry across the street to the hooker hotel as I shouted assurances. "I'll stay right here, Jerry. Make sure you don't get rolled."

Jerry rushed back and handed me his wallet, keeping a twenty for the lady and a ten for the twenty-minute room. A garish yellow and red sign atop the Hotel Califia and Bar blinked "Tecate" in medieval lettering as Jerry opened the door, where I glimpsed an office the size of a closet where a pimp sat chewing gum, watching TV, and collecting ten-dollar bills.

Jerry plunked down a ten and disappeared up the stairs, led by his still rigid arm. I watched the gorgeous creature appear on the second-floor balcony, guiding Jerry to an unmarked door where pleasure presumably lurked. During Jerry's twenty-minute absence, an unfortunate was beaten up outside the PARIS, a nightclub next door and down the block: someone knifed a guy. The *policia* appeared in seconds, hauling away his assailant. I walked over and inspected drops of blood on the sidewalk while keeping watch on the Califia Hotel balcony in case Jerry came flying over. I was jittery by the time Jerry stumbled down the stairs, turned in the key, and quietly crossed the street.

"So, how was she?" I asked. If he wasn't talking, I had my own stories.

Mumble, mumble. I focused on Jerry, and his freckles were pale. "So, what happened? I mean, it took you long enough." I glanced at a nonexistent watch.

"Well," he said.

I stared until he began, "We went upstairs." I'd seen that much.

"She took all her clothes off. Fine tits. Well, she didn't take off all her clothes. She kept on her little panties."

I continued staring, encouraging the reluctant Lothario.

He rubbed his face, and a few freckles reappeared. "She said, 'I'm no lady,' and I said, 'That's great because I don't cotton to ladies,' and she said, 'No, I'm really not.'"

I nodded encouragement.

"Well, I checked out the bikini panties and there seemed to be more of a bulge than was strictly necessary."

No siree. "You're kidding?" Of course, he wasn't.

"So... "

"So?"

"So, I got a blow job. "

Thereafter, the incident was referred to as *Crying Game II*, after the 1993 Academy Award winner for Best Picture, an episode I thought reflected badly only on Jerry.

My life had changed completely, such as patronizing laundromats. The one in Ensenada, unlike its U.S. counterparts, drew an upscale crowd. A white-haired man with salt and pepper stubble played harmonica for donations while two twenty-year-old *gringo* women prissily folded laundry, acting as if Mexican eyes might contaminate lacy undies. Ancient Maytag washers took quarters only, and the air was saturated with the sweet smell of detergent and fabric softener. I sat and read and gazed out the window at the park across the street where old men sat on benches and women pushed prams.

Time had lost meaning. Sextants and radar had replaced calendars and watches. The only guideposts were weather and whether I could find X part to complete Y project. Soon I would add whether there was too little or too much wind, having traded sailing for backed-up freeways and jury trials postponed at the last minute. I pedaled back to the boat through downtown, dodging cars and pedestrians, a spectacle for local merriment with laundry stacked two feet high behind my bicycle seat.

The Memorial Day weekend exploded with tourists. The locals said the invasion was smaller than the July Fourth or Labor Day weekends, but that was hard to believe. By noon on Saturday, the lines for Bananas Nightclub and Papas & Fritas were two blocks long. College and high school kids carried cases of

14

beer down the street while women paraded in bun-baring cut-offs and wore bosom-pooching halter tops with mind-boggling dimensions. The restaurants and hotel rooms were full of tourists leaning over balconies, inhibitions demolished by *cerveza* and tequila. By evening, many lay on sidewalks all over downtown.

By Sunday morning, the partygoers were in marginal shape. Several brushed their teeth on the street, while others slept on top of cars, mouths open, snoring. The boatyard crew reported two hundred *gringos* arrested. By noon, you couldn't walk on the sidewalks, but only in the street, outside of parked cars, dodging the bumper-to-bumper traffic dragging the main street, gagging pedestrians on exhaust fumes.

The next time Marty visited from Cardiff on the Sea, he brought his girlfriend, Vickie. We accepted the invitation of my new acquaintances, Kenny and Peggy, to join them for drinks on their monster, sixty-foot powerboat that had to cost well over a million bucks. After a dozen years of marriage, they enthusiastically despised each other. We sat in their luxurious cockpit and at first, they were entertaining, sniping and carping in luxurious misery. Kenny chain-smoked smelly cigars hated by Peggy, and she called him names while suggesting his increasing impotence, and Tanqueray poured freely. He was the king of Southern California avocados, and she was the heiress to a chain of mortgage banks, both unwilling to dismantle financial empires to purchase peace. I came away feeling good about *Grendel,* though it was inadequate even as a dinghy for their floating palace.

The boatyard decided to relaunch *Grendel* and finish the final work on the water. Launching required maneuvering into a ten-foot slip with a two-inch clearance between the dock and a large powerboat. The wind was gusting to twenty knots, creating a problem, at least for me. I'd owned *Grendel* for several years but had backed her into a narrow space only once. When backing, the propeller kicked her far to one side, but I'd forgotten which side.

Al, a friend from Scottsdale, had been marooned in Ensenada on a Northsea 27 and sensed this backing exercise might be worth watching. At the very least, it'd be a pleasant diversion during Al's four-month stay in Ensenada, which he had to wait out before he could sail his gorgeous Northsea 27 named *Ingrid* back to California. By taking delivery off-shore, he'd saved thousands of dollars in California sales taxes. Al had never captained a sailboat before and, after a rough trip to Ensenada, was deathly afraid of the voyage back to San Diego. I marveled at Al because, for a mid-sixties curmudgeon, he did great with the ladies. Forty-year-old April came down on weekends, did his laundry, satisfied his every appetite, I assume, and departed on Sunday afternoon. His Scottsdale main squeeze visited once a month.

My many colorful sailing stories had given Al an exaggerated sense of my seamanship, which was pathetically easy to embellish, based on a sailing resume of charters two or three weeks at a time, on boats I never had to see again. To Al, I sounded competent, taken in by the musings of a newly retired, but yet to recover lawyer. So, I tried backing *Grendel* among severe gusts and, according to Al, he suffered five near coronaries.

I missed the piling by the width of a scrape. The boatyard hands pushed me off another boat while *Grendel* bounced against the powerboat's fenders. So, I almost wiped out the dock. For some inexplicable reason, Al was impressed, perhaps at my survival. I was a little surprised myself, thankful no one found out about a worse mistake I'd made. After tying down the lines, I hopped back on board to shut off the engine and found it still in gear. They should have banned me from the seven seas. How could I avoid criminal negligence? I was competent at a half dozen sailing skills, and ignorant of a thousand others. With repetition, I might reach marginal, assuming I lived that long.

My days at the boatyard were down to the last gasp, which is what I did when I saw the final bill, $2,000 over the estimated price. It took sixteen hours of rigorous negotiation to lower the bill to $1,400, and then I had to date the second $700 check a month later, already broke for June.

I was leaving Ensenada three weeks after I'd planned. The day before leaving, I rode my bike into a rusty I-beam and punched a hole in my forehead. The collision sent a tingling arpeggio up and down my spine and I thought I'd broken my neck. I sat stunned in the sweltering Ensenada sun, wondering whether I'd be able to walk back to the boat, much less sail it somewhere. I swabbed the blood off and Al smeared an antibiotic in a hole that required a four-inch patch, and I stumbled around, wondering if this was an omen. I'd have to place an ad in the newspaper: "Crew urgently needed with journeyman electrical and mechanical skills, preferably curvaceous." I definitely needed help.

2

And So, It Begins

Robin and Hilda on their Coronado 28 asked me to buddy-boat with them to Cabo and with my lack of mechanical skills, I was more than willing. Hilda was a friendly Mexican woman of forty, a former Spanish teacher in Los Angeles, and Robin was an enigma. He was a skinny, blond scarecrow who'd been married four times, making me feel like a piker with only two previous wives. Robin avoided the States because he didn't know how many wives he'd divorced, and owed the IRS $15,000. With no assets, I suggested the IRS wouldn't bother him in the U.S., much less in Mexico.

I decided my dreamt-of circumnavigation officially began when I anchored in a hundred-yards-wide horseshoe cove protected from the long Pacific swells by the island of Todos Santos Sur, nine miles off the Mexican coast. Dozens of seabirds swooped around the thousand-foot crest of the three-mile-long, sun-drenched island, which I'd explored two years before and found covered with succulents. Millions of seagulls squawked the second I stepped ashore. I hiked for an hour to reach the highest point, lambasted by what sounded like a Donald Duck cartoon on steroids and rewarded with a panoramic view of Ensenada Bay. Fog shrouded the southern half.

Todos Santos Norte and Sur

I watched from the top of the island as Robin and Hilda sailed in. They anchored *Seaquest* far more gracefully than I'd anchored *Grendel*, which was why I'd sailed in first. When I arrived, fishermen were eating lunch on two pangas, drinking beer, and chattering away. I motored around the cove four times, trying to decide where to drop anchor, fretting about possible wind shifts, and worried the anchor would drag. My main emotion was scared shitless. What if my new anchor was crappy, like the one I'd suffered during a three-week charter in the Greek Islands? That anchor had dragged everywhere, including Mykonos Harbor. My buddy Morgan and I had to dive off the dock and scramble aboard to save the forty-five-foot Hardin from shipwrecking onshore.

I hadn't tested Grendel's new primary anchor before and was afraid of an embarrassing end to my often-bragged-about circumnavigation. The anchor was a new type neither I nor anyone I'd met was familiar with. But the anchor held like a charm and I frittered away the rest of the day, the way non-cruisers think of sailing. Of course, any anchor would have held in the utterly calm conditions with little wind, no surge, and no swell.

At 6 a.m., I was raring to begin the great adventure and sail down the coast when *Seaquest* radioed she wouldn't be ready for another hour. When we pulled up anchor, I almost drifted into *Seaquest*. I was too busy on the bow, sliding anchor chain into the hawsehole instead of watching where *Grendel* was floating off to.

"Sorry about that," I yelled at Robin as he and Hilda prepared to fend off, but we didn't touch. First close call. We headed out to sea, and that was the last time I saw *Seaquest*, fading into the fog behind me.

Two minutes later the radio squawked but I was up to my ears in busy and couldn't hear Robin over the engine noise. I stared into the cottony fog, which would have required x-ray vision to make sure the rocks off the south point of Ensenada Bay weren't lurking right in front of me. Unfortunately, I was still unfamiliar with the GPS, which the Defense Department jammed in the 1990s, reducing accuracy to a hundred yards. Defense Department jamming theoretically kept the Soviet Union from using GPS to aim missiles and obviously assumed the explosive power of the USSR arsenal would cover less than a hundred yards. The Coast Guard responded by building land stations to correct the Defense Department jamming, at little cost to the taxpayer compared to the total military budget.

I dropped into the cabin and grabbed the radio. "Be right with you, Robin. Give me a minute." He said something that sounded like his Loran, an almost obsolete predecessor to GPS, wasn't working. I fiddled with the GPS and compared it to the chart. I seemed to be on course.

"Come on back, Robin." No answer.

Al came on the radio, which he'd been doing the last twenty hours. He was ten miles away in Ensenada and still within radio range, but a world away in the claustrophobic fog. "Can't read Robin no more," he said.

"Come on back, Robin," I repeated. Not even static, and I was already up to my eyebrows in crises, having sailed about a mile with eight hundred miles left to Cabo San Lucas. I flipped the GPS back on, unsure how long it'd last on four AA batteries, but I had four sets of rechargeable batteries on standby. I was alone and petrified, in no mood to talk to Al.

I'd barely gotten started when the next near-disaster hit, or barely missed. The rocky point on the south entrance to Ensenada Bay rose out of the fog, and *Grendel* missed the rocks by two measly feet. I'd set the GPS for the rocks off the south entrance to the bay, realizing too late that I shouldn't aim for rocks. I should aim to miss the rocks. I counted these near-miss rocks and almost drifting into *Seaquest* as two near disasters on my first day, making me exceedingly jittery. I couldn't get used to the new radar unit and was having difficulty deciphering what seemed like an upside-down picture.

With a typical following wind, it's usually fairly easy to sail from Ensenada to Cabo. However, at *Grendel*'s average speed of five knots per hour, making 125 nautical miles a day, it'd take a week of dodging shrimpers at night and watching the radar 24/7 while sleepless and courting perpetual disaster. Great way to see the world, which I'd seen damn little of so far, surrounded by unending rollers and blanketing fog.

I was sailing blind with Mexican shrimpers looming out of the mist, navigating by steering away from eerie sounds emanating from unknown locations. Naturally, the fog grew thicker, reducing visibility to inches. I'd never sailed in fog before and it gave me a stomachache. One slip-up and everything I owned would disappear, including me.

Another engine reverberated somewhere to starboard, or maybe port. It was impossible to tell in the warm and clammy fog, now thick as pudding. I figured the other vessel wouldn't be off the port side where the rocks were. That's when I heard something in the cabin below, looked down, and saw water bubbling over the floorboards. We were sinking.

After the panic recounted in the first chapter, checking all the through-valves and compartments, I snatched up the floorboards and stared at the ankle-deep water. Instead of pumping seawater out, the bilge pump was siphoning seawater inside. Notwithstanding the fog, which I understood meant no wind, a light breeze had pushed the bilge outlet underwater. With *Grendel* slightly heeled, the bilge pump was pumping water back in as soon as it stopped pumping water out, developing a serious sucking sound as the entire Pacific Ocean tried to rush inside. I charged up the gangway into the eerie fog and hung over the side, checking the outlet. Yep, underwater. Back below, the floorboards were six inches under. Another few inches and *Grendel* would sink.

I ran back below, grabbed a plastic Ziplock and a No. 2 pencil, dashed topside, and hung over the side to jam the plastic-wrapped pencil into the hull outlet, hanging upside-down from the lifeline by my knees with my arms, shoulders, and head under the rushing water. A big black shrimper cut across the bow as I slid back on deck, and I jerked the tiller to the right, almost snagging shrimping nets that would have fatally entangled us. As the shrimper charged ahead, vanishing in the fog, I realized I only had to throttle down and reduce speed or change course to raise the outlet above the waterline. Either would have stopped the leak. Live and learn. Or, in my case, happy to live and perhaps learn another day. Revelation on day one of my around-the-world adventure: I was incompetent.

This episode freaked me out so much that I re-plumbed the bilge into the galley/kitchen sink, plugging the outside outlet so a suction would be impossible to develop. Though it made perfect sense at the time, looking back on it, diverting bilge water into the kitchen sink was disgusting. I'd lost count of the close calls on my first morning, literally at sea.

Though often inept and clumsy, I've always been a lucky bastard. The bastard part was straightforward. I was adopted. The lucky part began with my earliest memories. At age five, I uncovered a rattlesnake den on the Colorado cattle ranch where I grew up. I watched them slither away and was sternly warned by the parents to avoid diamondbacks forevermore. At age six, I began walking two miles to a one-room country school, pocketing souvenirs on the way home, chunks of bright yellow rock I found along the road. The parents saw my burned legs and shrieked. Carnotite, high-grade uranium ore mined a few miles up the road, radiation burns. Don't do that again either.

My list of happy escapes was almost endless. At age seven, I fell through the ice on the ranch reservoir. I couldn't swim but somehow escaped, arriving home sodden, shivering, and frozen. My survival amazed my parents. I don't know how I survived either but I can still conjure a hazy sheet of ice overhead.

At age eight, I dared a neighbor boy to rope me off my trusty white horse named Blaze. I galloped by and he neatly threw a lariat around my neck. I crashed to the ground, kerflop. Neck burns, no breaks. Parents again amazed.

At age nine, Blaze's saddle turned, and she kicked the crap out of it. That was my fault, being too puny to cinch the girth properly. Luckily, I'd fallen to the side without catching my foot in the stirrup.

On a trip to California at age ten, I ran pell-mell into an Arizona cactus, sprouting a pincushion of thorns. By then dad was used to my antics and tried not to laugh as he teased stickers out with a pair of pliers.

I thought captaining charters all over the world would make me a competent sailor. After all, few sailors survive becoming lost in the stormy Bermuda Triangle where howling winds shredded my mainsail, twisting and tossing the boat like a tilt-a-whirl. We climbed ten-foot waves, plunging headlong into troughs. Everyone except me lay too seasick to steer. My only sailor-like talent was immunity to seasickness, and we eventually blundered into the safety of Bimini.

After almost sinking *Grendel*, I was exhausted, dropping anchor in a picturesque bay off Point Colnett. After a single day, I was fed up with cruising.

Colnett Point was formed by a thousand-foot-high rock in layers of red and black, ten miles in circumference, but it offered no protection from rolling ocean waves and surge. Still, the sun was out, the sun shower was hot, and the Suns/Bulls NBA Finals' game began three minutes after I finished a deck shower. But nothing helped my mood. Why was I on a small sailboat by my incompetent self? Would I survive? These questions were compounded by frustration with the radar. I couldn't figure out the seemingly upside-down screen and couldn't find a control button to flip it right-side up. Impatient after five minutes, I gave up trying to figure it out.

After a sunny and clear beginning, the morning turned scary. I trusted the new anchor because the lighthouse hadn't moved, but I was too busy raising the anchor and stuffing the chain into the hawsehole to notice the surf grabbing at *Grendel*, pulling her dangerously close to shore. Shades of Todos Santos. I glanced up as surf swept the bow, ran back to the tiller, and revved the engine in reverse. The engine, of course, died. I sat with dreams of escape fading. One punch of the starter with the engine half warmed up, however, and we were back in business, reversing as fast as I could go as breakers nudged the bow.

Re-anchoring in the bay was another dangerous move. The ocean began twisting and gyrating like a berserk roller coaster, making *Grendel* jump around like a deranged kangaroo. The long swells were from storms thousands of miles away in Japan or Alaska. By the time they reached this distant shore unimpeded, they'd puffed up over ten feet high. We schussed up and down, scrambling everything I'd so poorly packed below.

The long rollers of green water thundered like cascades of giant dominoes, but the stern lifted daintily for each. Though no seawater came aboard, the motion was nauseating. The obvious solution was a stern anchor, the Danforth I'd already rigged, ready to go, displaying a modicum of seamanship. I let fifty feet off the bow anchor, dropped the Danforth anchor off the stern, and took up fifty feet on the bow. The Danforth anchor stopped us from riding so high. This lasted only five minutes before the shrieking I hadn't been able to identify turned into a crash, and I was back on a wild and woolly roller coaster. I tugged on the Danforth stern anchor and it came up easily. The surge had sheared off the steel endplate, rendering the anchor useless. One of my two primary anchors lost. My third anchor was for emergencies only, an ultra-heavy plow that required two people to lift out of the bilge and drop over the side, purchased when I thought Mary was coming along. It was so heavy it'd take a heavy winch to raise from the ocean floor. What could go wrong next?

I set the Tillermaster autopilot on a southerly course and collapsed in the cockpit, heart thumping as the stately old lighthouse faded behind. Then a forest of kelp appeared, waving under the keel so I jumped up and grabbed the tiller, hand-steering to dodge bulbous tendrils that would otherwise foul the prop.

After the first twenty-four hours, I wondered whether I should have stayed home. But I no longer had a home. I'd sold it and everything in it, hoping to see the entire world or die trying. I was tired of my job, dealing with stuffed-shirt lawyers, humorless judges, and cheapskate clients. Bugaboos included billing six-minute increments in private practice and the snarly politics and bureaucracy at the Attorney General's Office. Only a burning curiosity about the rest of the world kept me going through twenty-four years of law-related tedium. I traveled at every opportunity, cashing in frequent flier miles earned from a myriad of cases around the country, captaining charters in Turkey and Greece, to most Caribbean islands, Mexico, and Canada.

Hardin 45 charter boats in Athens: Mary and I background left

Beginning with graduation from law school in 1969, I spent summers traveling. My first wife and I drove around for three months in Europe, buying a VW Campervan at the factory in Wiedenbruck, Germany, and driving through East Germany. We checked out the Berlin Wall and ferried up to Denmark, meandering down through The Netherlands, Belgium, and France to Spain and Italy for a great first adventure. For twenty years I'd spent two- and three-week vacations sailing, less than coincidentally, involving many narrow escapes. I stepped on a shark in Belize and may have set a hundred-yard swimming record back to the boat, practically running on water. I later found it was an innocuous nurse shark. Most sharks, except for great whites, are similarly harmless.

Sailing full-time meant splitting with Mary. We'd made a plan to save every penny and retire early, aiming to quit before my fiftieth birthday. I beat the deadline by a few weeks but Mary couldn't leave the rat race without more savings in her retirement kitty. Weathering the split with Mary made for a rough six months before I left. We were both heartbroken. I wouldn't give up my dream, and she didn't have enough money to retire.

Mary in Bermuda

So, here I was, celebrating the single life. Eating soup out of a pan, listening to whatever music I wanted, and occasionally writing, when I could find the time.

I finally realized that with over seven hundred miles to Cabo, I didn't have enough fuel. Another item I'd forgotten to stock up on before leaving Ensenada. Though the wind was steady and I could easily sail, I had to run the engine at night to avoid fishing boats running without lights, a hazard I'd never heard of before leaving Ensenada. Fuel was available at only two places in the next seven hundred miles: San Quintin, coming up soon, or Bahia de Tortugas, aka Turtle Bay, about halfway down the outside of the Baja. San Quintin was the only possibility.

I'd driven through San Quintin a few years before and knew about a fishing camp accessible from the ocean, five miles from town, isolated by a road that was a disaster of rocks and ruts. San Quentin offered the best anchorage on the Baja, sheltered by a ten-mile-long sand spit protecting a long interior lagoon. In 1888, American land speculators sold San Quentin land to English speculators, describing the area to gullible investors back home as capable of "holding all the fleets of Europe put together." Puffery, because most of the lagoon dried at low tide. The English were gung-ho developers, dredging the harbor, building a flour mill and fifteen miles of railroad, planning to ship wheat and flour to Yuma, Arizona, over a hundred miles northwest. They abandoned the scheme in 1892.

I dropped the hook inside San Quentin bay, a hundred yards offshore in twenty-five feet of the calmest water I'd seen in years, like sitting in a goldfish bowl. There wasn't a sound, no lines slapping or water lapping at the hull. To the north sat five cinder cones, far across the lagoon, looking exactly like perfect volcanoes should look. The sandbar stretched across the western horizon with the open ocean two miles south. As the sun sank behind this travel poster, the sky turned pink from horizon to horizon, blazing the volcanoes into fiery-coned Mayan temples. I felt I'd earned every second of this gorgeous solitude, yet I was unappreciative, worrying about the lack of fuel. *Grendel*'s ancient Atomic 4 gasoline engine had been standard equipment on boats made in the 1960s and early '70s, and its gas mileage sucked. I'd spend as long as it took, finding fuel tomorrow.

As the sun rose, I made a leisurely breakfast and figured out the radar. The top of the radar wasn't north, like on maps and charts. The top of the radar screen showed the direction the boat was headed, which for me was south. The solution was too simple to believe, leading me to again question my competency. At least I'd solved one problem, happily sitting in the cockpit, occasionally joggled by noisy pangas returning from a night of fishing.

The first problem was getting ashore. The closest town was through breaking surf ten miles across the bay, which I couldn't cross without swamping the dingy. The only solution was to hail a fishing panga and pay the occupants to take me into town to buy fuel, which began a remarkable adventure.

I stood on deck, shouting *hola* at passing pangas. The occupants waved back. I grabbed a red five-gallon gas container and waved it at the next panga. The fishermen waved and turned to come alongside.

"Possible teine gasolina para mi barco?" I'd rehearsed this, asking if they had gas available for my boat, but without the gas can, they'd still be ignoring or staring at me. They waved me aboard, but I was disorganized, holding them off for five minutes while securing the dinghy on deck, trying to make *Grendel* look occupied. I hoped a dinghy on deck would make it less likely that someone would jump on board and steal thousands of dollars of electronics. Though I had five locks, none fit the door to the cabin and that set the tone for the day--unending worry about *Grendel* sitting alone, unprotected.

Most Mexican fishermen fished from a panga, built wide for buoyancy. This panga was driven by Frank, a Bronson-type, bow-legged chap with a humongous seventy-five-horse Evinrude. When I stepped on board it felt like creeping into an overheated slaughterhouse. A dozen headless mako sharks filled the panga, sloshing in a foot-deep pool of fish blood the length of a boat, which was also stuffed with nets reeking of fish guts and blood. Frank saw me staring at the pool of blood and began scooping it over the side.

The other fisherman introduced himself as Benjamin, motioning for me to sit next to him. I stepped over the sharks and sat on a filthy mat next to Benjamin. Frank flipped the seventy-five-horse Evinrude into gear, and we swooped away, planing immediately. Benjamin asked if I was by myself on the boat, and I began worrying in earnest. Would *Grendel* survive until I returned, assuming I ever did?

We snaked through a tortuous five-mile-long channel, arriving at the fish camp at 9:30 a.m. The camp sat a hundred years from a small volcanic cone in the center of five and stank of fish guts, nauseating, repulsive, and loathsome, fully appreciated only with smell-a-vision. Naked preschool boys and older boys in filthy shorts roamed between the sewage-coated lagoon and the camp, rolling in scabrous dirt, sand, and dust, chasing each other around the grimy lagoon. Squeaky-clean girls sat demurely in prissy dresses or shorts with colorful blouses, staying out of the boys' way while intently watching their every move. The women remained inside, out of sight, though I glimpsed two watching the children from afar and spying on the *gringo*. Four of the shacks had one window eight inches square. Six others had no windows and all were built from junk, scraps, and refuse.

31

The fishermen offered me a seat on lava rocks, flanked by three derelict cars. A dapper fuel deliveryman arrived in a new Toyota pickup, wearing white Reeboks, sharply pressed jeans, and a plaid shirt rolled to the elbows. He negotiated the sale of gasoline and oil mixtures for the fishermen's outboard motors. This took more than an hour, embroidered with wild tales graphically illustrated with the gestures of a dozen men caked in fish filth divvying up a sixty-gallon barrel of fuel.

I sat bored stupid, kicking dirt with my topsiders, saying *"no problema"* every time Frank and Benjamin promised we'd be leaving in only ten minutes to fetch *Grendel's* sorely needed fuel. They kindly agreed to charge me a mere fifty pesos, less than seventeen dollars for the round trip into town. Too bad I couldn't make do with outboard motor fuel.

I wandered around for another hour while the fishermen cleaned themselves up, shucking off bloody yellow foulies and tossing sharks into a community cooler that consisted of two large boxes filled with blackened ice. Promptly at noon, two and a half hours after coming ashore, they removed a battery from a panga and fitted it into a ramshackle Datsun pickup identifiable only by the imprint of a nameplate rusted off decades before. I stuffed three five-gallon gas cans in the back of the pickup, next to a hefty, headless mako shark they were taking to town to trade.

I crammed into the truck cab with three fishermen. Goat drove, a stubby chap prone to graphic hand gestures illustrating infinite longings for the female sex, bouncing between the blinding dust of the ditch and the vertebrae-collapsing, head-bumping corduroy of the road, covering us with dust that filled our lungs. I'd driven the road a year before and it'd taken me an hour, driving slowly to

32

avoid destroying my van. The road was so bad I never made it to the fish camp, though the fishermen made it to town in twenty jouncy minutes.

I asked what they wanted to trade the shark for and Benjamin said, "Marrywanna," rolling the R and making it sound magical. He asked whether I enjoyed that particular vegetable matter, and though I smoked with friends, these guys didn't qualify, so I smiled and denied using the stuff.

The first stop was at a *friend's* house in an alley off Highway 1, a faded pink duplex whose owner was absent, according to a bedraggled twenty-something mother of three who lived next door.

El Capitan Frank gave me the evil eye said intensely, "Pay me now." I handed over fifty pesos and said, "This includes everything, right? Back to the boat? Everything?"

"Well, sure. Yes," said Captain Frank.

I asked why they didn't leave the stinky shark with the neighbor lady, but they pretended not to understand. They kicked me out of the cab and I rode in the back of the truck where shark blood soaked my yuppie topsiders and I sat overpowered by the stench of rotting fish in the sweltering sun.

After half an hour, they spotted their missing friend cruising the main drag in a shiny, customized red truck with darkly tinted windows. He took the shark in trade, handing over a tinfoil-wrapped ounce of marrywanna for a hundred pesos, aka thirty-three dollars.

El Capitan unrolled the foil, and the fishermen began smoking lickety-split, freshening the dusty air with pungent resin. By the time we coasted into the center of town my companions were ripped, which made me happy because that made them far less menacing. They stopped at a bar, voting unanimously that I should buy a round of *caguamas*, liters of beer. A *caguama* cost a dollar at a supermarket and two dollars at a neighborhood Mexican bar, but this bar charged five bucks each. We sat, serenaded by a hundred-decibel jukebox wailing traditional Mexican music.

I coaxed them out of the bar and bought a few groceries while they drank a twelve-pack of Tecate beer. They insisted on stopping at a liquor outlet where I was ordered to buy eight cold *caguamas* for the hot dusty trip back to the fish camp. I drank one, and they finished the other seven, exhausting most of the marrywanna.

Having paid for the fuel to town, I claimed a share of the marrywanna, finally relaxing, puffing away while filling my gas cans at the Pemex, where no one seemed to worry about smoking at Mexican gas pumps. At 2 p.m. we jounced back to the fish camp, far more cheerful than when we left.

My three companions and several others retired to the end of the village with a liter of tequila, two twelve-packs of Tecate, and the rest of the pot. I watched a ten-year-old catch a three-foot shark, tie a line around its tail, and terrorize the girls while their mothers watched from shadowy doorways. Benjamin invited me to join the partiers, offering me the height of luxury, a chair. I declined everything except a cold Tecate. At 4 p.m., they promised I'd be back on *Grendel* in twenty minutes. I sat staring at the horizon, where *Grendel* might still be.

At 5 p.m., the village broke for supper. At 6, all the fishermen except Benjamin left in their pangas. They'd assigned me to Benjamin, who wasn't leaving because he could barely walk. With the amount of beer, tequila, and pot he'd imbibed, I was amazed he could even stumble. By then I was stone-cold sober.

Benjamin explained that the further delay was waiting for bait, though I suspected a conspiracy to savage *Grendel*. Would they leave me forever homeless in a boondocks fish camp in the Baja wilderness? I sat staring wistfully at the horizon, wondering if *Grendel* was still out there. Had it all been a conspiracy to steal the GPS, radar, HF radios, VHF radios, computer, TV with built-in VCR, printer, and more?

At 6:30, Benjamin drunkenly waved me aboard a panga, revved up the huge Evinrude, and hit the gas before changing his mind. Erratically, he reversed to the anchorage, grabbed a flag from another boat, and transferred the flag to his mast. He mumbled unintelligible things as we began again, cutting across the lagoon at high tide. Ten minutes later, we arrived at a peacefully bobbing *Grendel*.

Benjamin wanted to come on board for one last beer. I was so relieved at *Grendel's* pristine condition that I agreed, thinking it best not to antagonize an already surly drunk. Benjamin tromped his bloody waders into my pristine cockpit and I yelled at him to get the fuck off the boat. He was exceedingly hurt. The big clunk stood there sheepishly, pulling off his boots and tossing them into the panga. One beer, he said. Well, okay, just one. I ran below and grabbed a beer, determined to confine him to the cockpit.

He took tiny sips, in no hurry to leave. So, I set up the sun shower, the second reason I was anxious to get back to *Grendel*. I needed a relaxing hot shower after this filthy day from hell. Benjamin said, "Go right ahead," in perfect English, smiling, swilling his beer, perhaps thinking about demanding another one.

35

Like a dummy, I called his bluff. *"Mi bano. Esta usted para pescado?"* This was intended to mean, "I'm taking a shower so bug off and go catch some fish." He sat there, smiling vacuously, but I figured he'd have to leave when I began my shower.

Like an idiot, I set out the shampoo, soap, and a towel, shucking off my clothes below, emerging topside, bare-assed naked. Benjamin's smile turned to a grin, tongue hanging out like he'd been planning this scene for eight hours, ever since I'd told him no one else was on board, meaning no female company. He started grabbing at my bare white butt as I stood in shock for an entire split second. I slapped his hands, stopping him from unzipping his pants and illustrating rampant desires.

Benjamin not only wouldn't leave but insisted on showing me that which I had never, ever wanted to see. He was in a frenzy such as I'd never known. He had to be nuts. I'd given him no encouragement that I knew of. Plus, I was fifty years old to his thirty and far from the body-beautiful Schwarzenegger type. Illustrating his remarkable lack of good taste, I was more of a skinny twig. I screeched for him to get the hell off my boat and into his panga, fending him off, stopping him from hauling out his wanger and shucking off his pants as he graphically illustrated intentions for my milky white body.

After screaming him back into the panga, I collapsed in a heap, mixing a monster gin and tonic as he roared away. I was happy to have enough fuel to make the 250 miles to Bahia Tortuga, assuming I didn't have to motor more than a few hours each night. I slept fitfully, locking the outside doors, knowing Benjamin was lurking out there somewhere in a panga with his flag up.

36

The sail down to Bahia Tortuga, aka Turtle Bay, taught me to listen with every molecule of my body. I honed an instinct for any unfamiliar noise, change in tone, volume, or frequency that would mean another emergency, a slapping halyard, fidgety spinnaker pole, or rattling anchor chain. My greatest fears were any of three alarms signaling excess water in the bilge, low fuel, or leaky propane. Propane, because it's heavier than air, is highly dangerous on watercraft. Amid this learning process, I forgot one of *Grendel*'s most crucial maintenance requirements, and it remained undiscovered until two weeks later while motoring from Cabo to La Paz. But that was a disaster that was a long time off. Others lurked on the way to Cabo.

BAJA CALIFORNIA (NORTE)

1. Tijuana
2. La Rumorosa
3. Mexicali
4. Ensenada
5. Laguna Hanson
6. Cañon de Guadalupe
7. Santo Tomás
8. Valle la Trinidad
9. Llano el Chinero
10. Camalú
11. Parque San Pedro Martír
12. San Felipe
13. San Quintín
14. Puertecitos
15. El Rosario
16. Bahia San Luis Gonzaga
17. Punta San Carlos
18. Cataviña
19. Isla Angel de la Guarda
20. Punta Prieta
21. Bahía de los Angeles
22. Santa Rosalillita
23. El Barril
24. Guerrero Negro
25. El Arco

Enlarged Area
Area Amplificada

Baja California (Norte)

Baja California Sur

Baja California Norte—Turtle Bay/Bahia Tortuga (below No. 26)

I was happy to anchor near a whitewashed lighthouse on the highest point of picturesque San Jeronimo Island. Unlike the camp at San Quentin, the lighthouse overlooked a spiffy fish camp with houses that looked like escapees from a 1950s American tract development, trim clapboard with windows symmetrically placed. It must have been run by women. When the sun set, the wind piped up to thirty knots and swells wrapped around the island, making *Grendel* pitch and jerk all night long, a truly miserable anchorage.

38

Morning brought my first long crossing, a hundred miles across the Bahia Sebastian Vizcaino, where gray whales flocked every year from January to March, breeding in lagoons. I prepared for the crossing by cooking up a batch of spaghetti caliente, then *Grendel* began surfing down long ocean swells, cutting spaghetti prep short. I marveled at the zombie Tillermaster violently see sawing through sixty degrees, keeping the course a hell of a lot better than I could have done by hand. The cross-seas would have left me exhausted in a single hour. If the Tillermaster blew its last fuse, I'd be hand-steering for a hundred hours, all the way to Cabo.

Turtle Bay was the only place to easily refuel, the prime stop for anyone sailing the eight hundred-mile-long Baja. It was the perfectly imagined bay, three hundred degrees enclosed by miles of mesas to the north, flat desert studded with volcanoes stretching east, and miles of rolling hills to the south, and far too spacious to protect against rambunctious winds.

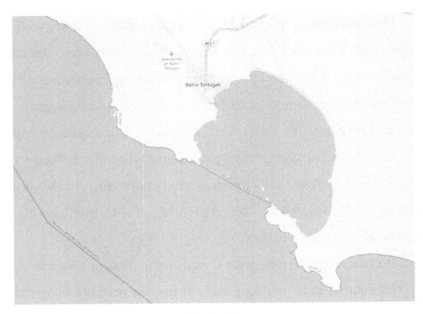

Turtle Bay

I arrived twenty-eight hours after leaving Isla San Geronimo, and the wind was blowing like snot. This was the first decent sailing since Ensenada, so I shut off the engine and majestically sailed into the ten-mile-long bay where hassles built toward disaster. I'd read about the dangerous hundred-yard-long fuel dock, a monstrosity more fully appreciated eight hours later. I sailed in gingerly, not knowing what to expect.

The dock was constructed with rusty steel girders fifteen feet high, much too high for me to tie up to and fatal to rub against. The slightest wind shift would drive a boat into rusty rebar, which chomps fiberglass. A fuel line ran the hundred-yard length of the dock. To refuel, you had to anchor at the end. I circled for twenty minutes, waiting for someone to appear. When no one did, I anchored, which was the apparent signal for the fuel lady to show up. She yelled something I couldn't hear, so I pulled up a hundred feet of chain and motored in close for intimate conversation.

She insistently motioned me to re-anchor next to the dock, but I couldn't tell the depth of the water and was morbidly afraid of going aground. A previous incident in San Diego, anchoring in too shallow water, almost damaged the keel.

Half the town gathered to watch as I concentrated on the depth meter, powering next to the rusty dock. When I got in position, I threw *Grendel* in slow reverse and ran forward to drop the anchor. But before I could release the anchor, *Grendel* drifted away from the dock. I had to try anchoring three times in front of half the town. Then, after shouted exchanges, the fuel lady said only diesel was available.

Local boys begged for money when I stepped ashore. I'd stuffed my pockets with candy, which several accepted instead of money. I then walked a mile to the Pemex gas station with five gasoline containers, guided by bribed children. The gas station only had unleaded gas and *Grendel* required regular. The gas station attendant said regular gas was scheduled for delivery at 8 a.m. the next day, and I wondered if he might also have a bridge for sale.

I left the gas cans at the gas station and the kids took me to an outdoor market for fresh fruit and veg, available only in shades of brown and overripe. Then to a restaurant for a break from my limited culinary skills. The restaurant was excellent, and I got back to the boat in time to listen to the Bulls/Suns NBA Finals and that dang Michael Jordan forced the Bulls to beat the Suns by three points.

Before going to bed, I surveyed the dock for potential hazards. In case of a wind shift, a panga anchored between *Grendel* and the dock should stop her

41

from rubbing against rusty rebar. But at midnight, I awoke to the God-awful sound of crunching fiberglass. I rushed naked on deck to find *Grendel* had drifted under the dock, wedging the mast-top radar underneath. The gentle swells bobbed *Grendel* up and down, crushing the radar unit under the dock. I cried salty tears, pounding fists on the cabin top, dancing up and down, screaming and yelling and cursing and howling at my stupidity.

How could I cruise around the world when I was unable to sail for a single week without destroying a $2,000 radar unit? Replacing the radar unit wasn't remotely in my budget. The panga failed to stop me from drifting under the dock because the wind had died instead of shifting. Without the tug of the wind on the anchor, the heavy chain pulled *Grendel* forward and under the dock. In the blackest frame of mind I could remember, I re-anchored twice, the second time a long way away from the dock and the hundred other boats in the harbor, desperately needing to be alone. Perhaps forever. I should have re-anchored far away from the dock before going to bed.

Losing the radar reduced my chances of survival. I'd have to dodge fishing boats during the week it'd take to sail to Cabo, unable to nap more than fifteen minutes at a time. With radar, I opened one eye to check the screen and then went back to sleep, a trait perfected by sailors worldwide. Now I'd have to stay awake night and day, with an occasional daytime nap.

I took the radar dome apart the next morning. The dock had compressed the cover and broken the swiveling circuit board, a catastrophe of relatively minor proportions, except for one wrinkle. The unit would have to be shipped to the States, and I later found it'd take forever to get it back because all imports into Mexico were routed through Mexico City. If parts arrived at all, they often took months, and exorbitant customs fees doubled the cost.

Only because gasoline was dripping down my elbow, I noticed the carburetor had broken off the outboard and dangled off a quarter-inch gasoline line. This resulted in another round of cursing and screaming. Would I learn enough to survive to Cabo, or was I too lazy and inexperienced to anticipate potential hazards before I did the next stupid thing? I couldn't afford to continue like this, financially or mentally. Ah, the carefree sailing life.

I landed the dinghy on the town dock, then went to fill the cans with regular gas--shocked to find it available when promised. I then took a taxi back to the dock. To refuel I had to haul five-gallon cans up and down a rusty, fifteen-foot-high ladder, filling *Grendel's* tanks with a funnel. Then I fell into bed, exhausted.

Though I was happy to get the hell out of Turtle Bay, the next morning's sail was a succession of errors. The first disaster struck when I sailed off the anchor. The mainsail jibed and threw the boom swiveling across the deck. I ducked just in time to keep it from knocking off my head, but the sudden twist of the boat bent the piston that powered the Tillermaster. Instead of perfectly straight, it was now an unlovely U-shape. I needed to rest before trying to straighten the Tillermaster shaft, so I wasted an hour fiddling with bungee cords, trying to position the tiller to self-steer on a southerly course. No such luck.

So, I dropped the sails and let *Grendel* drift for five hours, hoping to sleep. But the swells were huge, rolling the boat without pause. I was so tired that my whole body tingled, and we were hours from the closest harbor. Another low point in the first week of my so-called circumnavigation, or the first 200 hundred miles of it. I had to run to the mast and yank the lines as fast as possible to set the course, and that made steering complicated. It only worked if I was headed directly into the wind. I would point her into the wind and run to the mast over the rolling deck, but by the time I got there, she would have swung off the wind, whiplashing the boom so hard it threatened to break. Without a boom, the mainsail would be worthless, flapping without a long, powerful arm to hold it down and catch the wind.

After five tries, I lost patience. The mangled Tillermaster lay on the cockpit cushions with a twisted arm of stainless steel. I gingerly approached, applying vice grips, but only dented the stainless tube. Without a vice on board, I couldn't figure out how to straighten the shaft. If I ever got it fixed, I vowed to treat the Tillermaster as the primary deity it was, God in metal.

When sailing by myself I had no time to do anything but rest in the cockpit and navigate. I needed another person on the boat for safety, and with little or no time to eat or clean, the boat was filthy. I spent hours drifting on rolling seas, trying to straighten the piston so it'd slide smoothly in and out of the Tillermaster. Without automatic steering, I'd have to hand-steer 24/7. I fast realized that only the Tillermaster kept me sane, avoiding unending hours in the cockpit in the rain and scorching sun, with no sleep or rest.

I unbolted the aluminum extension to the Tillermaster shaft and accidentally dropped the bolt on the cockpit floor. It rolled to rest next to a two-inch steel cockpit drain, and a flashbulb went off in my crippled brain. I secured the bolt and inserted the Tillermaster shaft into the drain, gently levering it roughly straight. Sighting along the length revealed a shape similar to the hind leg of a jackrabbit. I gave it another tug, and it looked more like a jackrabbit leg on backward. Hopefully straight enough for government work.

I put the Tillermaster back together and gingerly flipped the "on" switch. The shaft bucked and whirred, singing a song like a tone-deaf second-grader with adenoids. But it worked. I devoutly dropped to one knee, making the secret sign of the Tillermaster sect on my forehead, over my heart, and on my groin. May the one true God Tillermaster live forever. Genuflect, genuflect, genuflect.

During the four days to Cabo, I edged around the Tillermaster, never showing my backside lest I offend. It had saved my life, or at least many miserable, cold, wet, and exhausting hours in the cockpit. I paid it ridiculous compliments, praising the omnipotent deity as sublime, omnisteerant, and supreme phantom course finder, and dreamed of buying a backup God.

A notable fringe benefit of sailing was the failsafe single-handers weight-loss program, which could be marketed in the States for a fortune. This program would let you to eat anything you wanted, anytime you wanted, and you wouldn't gain an ounce. Of course, I never had time to eat, because of navigation, sail trim, catastrophic emergencies, and death-defying risks. This diet would put spice in the life of the average American, who would drop rolls of fat like lard on a griddle. Come Cabo I'd be scarfing down real ice cream, as opposed to the nonfat yogurt I'd eaten for mega-years. I dreamed of pizza with double dripping cheese as well as guacamole, and sour cream piled on baked potatoes--in fact, everything on the menu.

I was beat, having slept little after crushing the radar. The safest course was far from land, so I set sail far offshore to Cabo San Lucas, knowing it would take four more days if the wind held. Land only brought big-time trouble. I can't remember much about the days spent sailing to Cabo from Turtle Bay, but I only suffered a few near disasters. Thus, the trauma must not have been excessive, only the usual average kind of sailing trauma. I was fixated on arriving in Cabo, scarfing steaks and ice cream while getting the radar fixed, locating one and a half amp fuses for the Tillermaster, changing the oil, and looking for a new outboard motor after the carburetor had gone missing from the dinghy's outboard. How I hadn't a clue, but I should have known the worst disasters were yet to come.

The unending problems were depressing. I cried, missing Mary. Almost ten years invested in my best-ever relationship, poof, gone. Also, I'd never suspected I was borderline incompetent and now I wasn't sure it was borderline. I had to find someone to assist on the boat. Mary's last words were how much she loved me, but that had to be a lie. She'd backed out of coming on the boat though we'd been planning to do exactly that for years.

My only consolation was music, from classical to Billy Joel. I'd corresponded with women interested in sailing around the world but there weren't many adventurous ladies out there. I was content to sit in the cockpit with a gin and tonic, having found God, whose address was 774 W. 17th St., Costa Mesa, CA, etched on the end of the Tillermaster, where the formerly bent stainless steel shaft slid in and out every second. The first God I'd ever heard of who could steer a pitching, lurching boat, twenty-four hours a day.

On June 22 at first light I rounded Cabo Falsa, five miles from Cabo, feeling like the Prodigal Son, coming home to the harbor for the first time in days, two weeks out of Ensenada and out of sight of land. Time for a commemorative photo of the cape with my Minolta 35mm, which had taken ooh-aah pictures all over the world. Then I discovered another casualty of my negligence. When I'd rounded the cape, the camera crashed off the bunk onto the cabin floor. The photo I took of the cape was blotchy. Relaxing for a single second risked bankruptcy, if not croaking.

I leisurely sailed along the gold coast, from Cabo Falso past multi-million-dollar condos, fancy resort hotels, and the Cabo sea-arch, standing with the tiller in hand, in my ocean-going yacht. What a joke. I was a skanky miserable old buzzard, possessing neither dress whites nor a captain's cap with scrambled eggs. My pansy beard made me look like a victim of mange, and I'd scarred my knees genuflecting before the Tillermaster.

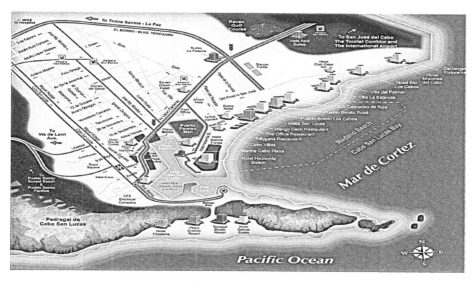

Cape Falso to Cabo San Lucas

Hotel Solemar was the closest resort to the arch. I'd climbed the highest hill above the arch the year before, taking a trail that began next to Hotel Solemar's veranda. Contrary to Swiss TV ads, I found it difficult to climb in

47

Birkenstocks. Recklessness eclipsed valor, and while trying to avoid mounds of human excrement next to the Catholic shrine on top, I almost fell eight hundred feet overlooking one of the world's most expensive fishing villages. In Cabo, Mary and I had always hung out in Eric Clapton's Giggling Marlin, where he no doubt giggled over the sheer volume of *gringo* dollars flooding into his bank account.

I swung around the sea-arch and almost rammed an ocean liner hauling anchor and headed toward my left elbow, a hundred times larger and ten times taller than *Grendel*. I suddenly understood why the captains of small sailboats never wear white. Brown stains can be difficult to remove.

I would have spun the wheel, but I didn't have one, so I rudely shoved God Tillermaster aside and flipped the tiller ninety degrees, finding myself on a tangential collision course instead. An object hogging the horizon like IMAX is difficult to avoid, and I damn near backed into the rocks behind me to escape the five-mile-wide path of the Love Boat. The gigantic ship acted as if it wanted to eat me for breakfast, for the sheer entertainment of its passengers, who stood on her decks, yawning at my imminent demise.

"Hey, Maude. Look at that tiny little sailboat down there. The one with the hobo on the

back."

"Yeah, Harold. Think he'll be able to get out of our way?"

"Shouldn't think so. Get the video cam going, stupid."

"Look at the way the wee thing almost turned over when it hit our bubbles. Bob and Carol

will get a real kick out of this."

"How is that funny-looking guy able to hang on while he's swirling around a whirlpool?"

The Love Boat's white, mountainous backside slid by, almost pushing me through the sea-arch backward. As the huge boat sailed away, Cabo San Lucas bobbed up and down in front of me and my palsied hand turned *Grendel*'s pointy end toward the harbor.

Ten years before, Cabo San Lucas had been a sleepy Mexican fishing village. By 1994, it was an expensive jet-setter destination with wall-to-wall resort hotels, yuppie gringo bars, and condos costing millions. Leonard, a single-handing German, received *Grendel* at the dock, helping my paralyzed self into a slip. Dock security appeared in the person of a sign-language-speaking Mexican wearing a blue and scarlet uniform with a matching, menacing riot baton. I agreed to present myself at the marina office within five minutes, whether I could walk, or not.

The sweet marina lady revealed the cost of a boat slip. Twice my daily budget. In the space of a heartbeat, my planned week in Cabo shrank to one night. A slip at the almost empty marina cost thirty-one dollars a day, the equivalent of sixty-five dollars in 2022. No wonder the marina was almost empty. Leonard told me that marina slips in La Paz were $300 a month, a tenth the Cabo price. I gulped my way back to the boat after paying an amount budgeted for three days, a one-day slip fee plus key deposit, collapsing for a restorative nap before venturing back into the shimmering Cabo sun.

Since I'd been in Cabo the year before, two more resort hotels had opened downtown and *gringos* wandered the streets in droves. I ducked into the Baskin-Robbins store for the air conditioning and ordered a fat-laden triple-scoop chocolate sundae with the works, an eight-dollar splurge. By the time I ate lunch and bought the *Los Angeles Times* to catch up on *gringo* land, I'd blown a week's allowance. If I didn't leave for La Paz in the next few hours, I'd have to write home for money, though I couldn't think of who I could put the bite on.

Leonard rescued me, introducing me to dollar fish tacos and happy hour margaritas in bars and restaurants all over town. We spent the next twenty hours drinking and walking around half-crocked, discussing weighty philosophical issues and solving world crises. Leonard planned to leave Cabo as soon as the port captain cleared him to leave. Unfortunately, the port captain hadn't shown up at work for three days. Leonard planned to sail three hundred miles offshore to Seattle, where he hoped to entice a comely damsel to join his world cruise, all while working on his spirituality.

"Say what?", I said, balancing the dregs of a potent margarita. "Pray tell, what is spirituality?"

I always asked for a definition of spirituality by anyone who uttered the word, having memorized the dictionary definition: devotion [to what?], holiness [in connection with which God or religion?], piety, saintliness, and sanctity.

Leonard lifted long fingers to order a drink, shaking the tightly bound gray ponytail that topped his immaculately dressed frame, and blinking pale blue eyes. "I would have asked that question a year ago. Now I am understanding."

The happy hour waiter took refill orders and I groaned, "What is it you understand?" Leonard launched into a devoted description of *The Urantia Reader*, later showing me this holy book in its place of honor aboard his compulsively neat forty-foot sailing machine, *New Dawn*. And the pious evening faded into the saintliness and sanctity of Margaritaville.

Leonard compounded my money worries. Imported marine parts had to clear customs in Mexico City, taking months to arrive and doubling in price by gathering layers of *mordida*, aka bribes. Mexican government bureaucracy, similar to many if not most governments, often took months and reams of paper to navigate. Importing parts without suffering bankruptcy required finding other cruisers driving down from the States. Cruisers helped each other out, knowing they'd be in the same situation on any given day. Thus flourished the informal import system, illicitly slipping boat parts into Mexico, based on one fact. Border guards seldom to never inspected the contents of cars and trucks driving down the Baja.

Downwind Marine and Pacific Marine Supply in San Diego administered the cruisers' pipeline, filling most orders from Mexico. Or you could take a bus or fly to the States and bring the parts down yourself. The cruisers' pipeline could take weeks but helped conserve the typically spartan cruising budget.

Onward to La Paz; expensive Cabo, sayonara. Leonard inspected *Grendel* and suggested I buy a thick rubber collar to secure the boom. This would prevent an accidental jibe, sending the boom flying across the cockpit when the wind unexpectedly changed direction, which happens often and had bent the Tillermaster into a U-shape. Without a collar to prevent an accidental jibe, the boom might break, rendering the mainsail inoperable and the boat out-of-control.

I left Cabo in high spirits, staring down a cruise ship bent on reversing into my path as *Grendel* glided away on a southwest wind, perfect for my initial easterly heading. Such idyllic conditions should have warned me the weather would soon explode in my face. As the sea-arch disappeared behind me, I soared on the following wind. Noon faded into night, and the wind shifted from the southeast, creating a cross-swell that jerked *Grendel* around like the Mad Hatter's tea party ride at Disneyland. By midnight, rolling green seas swept over both sides of the boat, drowning the cockpit where I sat huddled. The wind howled like a wolf, searching for a Little Red Riding Hood who seemed to be me, initially settling for the delicate God Tillermaster, which blew its next to the last fuse. And then *Grendel* jibed.

As predicted by Leonard twelve hours earlier, the mainsail swung across the cockpit, breaking the boom like a twig and missing my head by a whisker. Disaster. The sixteen-foot boom was transformed into an aluminum club, swinging wildly overhead, jagged and out of control. Without a boom to hold the mainsail taut, *Grendel* went berserk. And God was dead.

I fended off the aluminum club with one hand, somehow keeping it from taking my head off in chunks. With my other hand, I strained to unscrew the fuse box in the dead God while holding the flashlight and the tiller, trying to keep *Grendel* from her natural inclination to head toward the closest hazard, rock, or shore. Plus, I had to hunt for a line knife to cut the topping lift and lower the boom to the deck.

This disaster happened right after midnight, finding me in a soaked cockpit deserted by God. Without a stabilizing mainsail, *Grendel* hobby-horsed out of control. I only had one more fuse for the Tillermaster, and Leonard had told me a sad story: There were no one-and-a-half amp fuses available in Cabo, or anywhere in Mexico. The jagged boom had also poked a hole in my new $1200 mainsail, another victim of my retarded seamanship.

Could I declare bankruptcy at sea? With my average daily destruction of essential gear, I couldn't afford to go cruising. First thing in La Paz, I'd find an aluminum welder, assuming such a person existed. Mary was right, though she never came out and said so during our seventeen sailing charters all over the world. I was a slow-learning klutz who rushed into things, never slowing down to do things carefully. Simple self-preservation must have convinced her to back out.

The storm was unending, rolling over *Grendel* in sheets of black. I couldn't think or see, buried in cascading green water, trying to hang on until first light, half an hour before sunrise. A wave hit the flashlight, and it died. I had no spare, so I tied the tiller to my leg, freeing a hand to change God's fuse, working through problems one by one.

I changed batteries in the GPS, twice scrambling to pick AAs off the deck before they washed overboard. Where the hell were we? Only the GPS knew for sure, but the satellites refused to cooperate. With water lapping the floorboards, I flipped the switch to the bilge pump, which had failed to start automatically as advertised. Should I cut the mainsail down? What was holding it up? The boom had telescoped, halves swinging in unison, and I mourned the hole in the brand new mainsail, afraid I'd have to buy another one.

I inched along the deck toward the mast as I kept repeating, "Sailing is fun," intent on lowering the mainsail amid surging seas that whiplashed *Grendel* like a giant washing machine, black inside like death. When I untied the line to the mainsail, it wouldn't drop an inch. I peered through the darkness at the mast top. The line had gotten hung up, but there was no way I could climb the mast because the storm was swinging the mast top through a fifty-foot arc.

I clipped onto the jack line that would supposedly keep me tethered to the boat if a wave swept me overboard. However, I'd tied the jack line myself, and I tied crap knots. Though the mainsail was double-reefed with two-thirds wrapped around the boom like a carpet, as small as it'd go, I was petrified. Without keeping the mainsail up, I couldn't hold a course. Only the lazy jacks, which guided the mainsail to drop into accordion pleats, kept the whole mess from falling on the deck.

The catastrophe would never have occurred if I'd installed the thirty-five-dollar rubber snubber that Leonard suggested I buy at my first opportunity, but the Cabo marine store had been closed, and I'd been in a rush to leave. Though I'd never been so wet, I was lighthearted, feeling as one with the ocean and lucky the boom hadn't punched through the deck into the cabin below. The sky brightened to gray and pearled up, and I vaguely realized dawn was near.

The wind dropped, and the past faded as the churning black water turned a pleasant shade of blue. The massive cross-swell dropped to a chop, and little sports fishing boats darted from the mainland, passing close like skittering water bugs. The fishing boats were mighty curious or trying to run *Grendel* down, shearing off at the last second. It's common knowledge in the sailing community that powerboats were invented to give heart attacks to real sailors.

The boom-breaking storm had rolled *Grendel* between forty-five and fifty degrees on every wave, making a mess in the cabin. Closets and cupboards had emptied into a snarled mess. I surveyed the damage and again tried to lower the mainsail, but I couldn't find the proper line without a flashlight, even in the growing light. The Ensenada boatyard had installed the boom preventer too close to the mast, but that was my responsibility, rushing to La Paz without a preventer, unknown to me until mentioned by Leonard. Lesson learned?

I was zombified, having had no sleep, relieved when *Grendel* rounded the point at Bahia Ventana. A giant chess rook with red stripes guarded the point, a perfect lighthouse, a sentinel over an eight-mile curve of deserted powder beach. I sailed by the Hotel Arena and along the beach toward a wrecked freighter that had grounded years before, a mere skeleton evaporating to rust.

The anchor dropped into gently rolling water, twenty feet deep, and *Grendel* swung into the wind, facing the freighter. The lighthouse overlooked the Hotel Arena and rows of empty chaise lounges stretching south. A long-legged beauty with a wide-brimmed hat occupied one lounge, ostensibly reading. I dropped anchor and sat on the deck, focusing the binoculars to see whether the occupant of the chaise lounge was someone I'd recognize, such as a movie star. The Hotel Arena was reachable only by private plane, a haven for the rich and famous.

I must have invaded her privacy because the movie star escaped back to the hotel, perhaps to watch old reruns. *Grendel* was the only sailboat in the wide, long bay, bobbing on ripples sweeping hypnotically around the far-away point, exposing the sailing schtick as a classic love-hate relationship.

The crisp morning dawned with zero wind, the sea flat as a lake, and the sun warmed all it touched, turning the freighter from orange to red as I headed north toward La Paz. I balanced a mug of mint tea and a can of Mexican V-8 on the tiller, adding boiling water to a couple of packets of instant strawberry and cream oatmeal. The Tillermaster threaded a perfect line toward

Point Coyote, where I'd turn west and in a few miles and head south for Bahia de La Paz.

High thin stratus clouds stretched across the sky, forecasting a storm front that would hopefully wait until after I arrived in La Paz. I wore my camel driver's cap to keep off the killer sun, pouring water down my neck. My t-shirt was wet and wearable when smoke began pouring from the cabin below.

I ran down and unlatched the stairs to inspect the engine, finding smoke spiraling off the oil reservoir. Anxiously, I checked the oil, almost shorting out the engine. My clumsiness sent sparks up my arm and superheated the dipstick, which burned my fingers, making me drop it into the bubbling chemicals of the bilge. I had to instruct myself, "Dummy, put the oil in first."

The quart of oil I threw in the engine didn't cause an overflow so I straightened a wire hanger, wedging my head and shoulders inside the engine compartment to retrieve the dipstick from the bilge. Backing out, I brushed the bilge alarm, and it howled like the burglar alarm it originally was. With it wailing in my ears, I tried to concentrate on checking the oil. Total contents: one quart, the quart I'd just added. I topped the oil up with another one and a half quarts, which brought it up to the required two and a half quarts. I had run the engine dry while fending off multiple crises on the way down from Ensenada, forgetting to check the oil for two weeks.

The oil pressure spiked to ten out of the recommended minimum of forty-five and I slunk toward La Paz, the dumbest sailor on the planet. It seemed that cruising was too much for me to handle. How could I run out of oil? I hadn't checked it once during the hectic weeks from Ensenada to Cabo. Was I incompetent? The answers were depressingly clear. No wonder I was looking for a girlfriend.

I'd captained a dozen sailing charters with Mary accompanying me, and shit *always* happened, often in series. Such as two weeks sailing the Grenadines from St. Vincent to Grenada. The trade winds swept our rowing dinghy toward Central America with us in it. If we hadn't been buddy sailing with a just-met couple, who launched their dinghy to save us, we'd have been off on a Bligh-like voyage. The next day, a faulty bilge pump and leaky stuffing box threatened to sink the boat, which we barely escaped by the use of copious duct tape. Then we anchored too close to our buddy boat and a tidal surge smashed our boat against their bow, three incidents in the first twenty-four hours of the charter. I felt like the guy with a perpetual black cloud over his head, captive in Al Capp's Little Abner comic strip. Was I destined to be alone? Mary must have been preserving her sanity by bailing out on my so-called circumnavigation, but I couldn't go back now. I had nothing to go back to. Onward and downward, like the captain of the *Titanic*.

I was afraid I wouldn't make it to La Paz before sundown, the base of operations for several sailing charters I'd organized in the Sea of Cortez. The area north of La Paz ranks with the Virgin Islands as among the best cruising in the world. Always comfortable, except in summer when there's little wind and the sun melts the sea into the air, covering sailors with oceans of sweat--or for women, light perspiration.

Not only was the engine destroyed, but God Tillermaster, without warning, turned abruptly left. Either God had been injured or I'd encountered a weird magnetic disturbance. Leonard had given me the *Jack Williams Guide to the Sea of Cortez*, autographed by Jack Williams himself, and it mentioned a magnetic interference. Possibly God wasn't dead: long live God? Still, the oil pressure stayed at a pathetic ten and I could only putt-putt along at two knots an hour, still hoping to make La Paz by evening.

I crept through the channel between the peninsula and the magical islands of Espiritu Santo and Partita, north of La Paz, past the long fingers of the peninsula that form sheltered bays alive with fish, clams, and manta rays, diving pelicans, and killer whales. The gorgeous day sailing to La Paz ended when the engine died a half-mile from the La Paz marina, at dusk in the middle of a hundred anchored boats. I broke a record for the thirty-five-foot dash, running to the bow in seconds, throwing out the anchor as *Grendel* began to drift into the closest boat. The anchor held like super glue. Clunk, and we stopped on a peso.

The guy on the closest boat waved, apparently thinking I was his new neighbor. Slick. I'd radioed ahead to the marina, which had deployed people on the dock, awaiting *Grendel's* bowline. I radioed them to hang loose until I could get the engine restarted, thus alerting everyone on the two hundred boats in the La Paz cruising community that a newcomer named *Grendel* had broken its boom, needed assistance to dock, and its engine had died a few yards from the marina. Then the hapless captain had to throw out an anchor to avoid decimating the fleet. I must have sounded incompetent and exhausted, which I certainly was. A cruiser named *Taurus* offered to come aboard and help me dock, but I declined the offer.

It took fifteen minutes of grinding to start the engine, during which I considered staying on anchor overnight to recover from public embarrassment, but I couldn't stand the thought of being so close. Maria, the marina proprietress, and Terry, a self-pegged professional idiot, caught my lines, securing *Grendel* as I nosed into the slip closest to The Dock, the marina's bar and restaurant. Iron gray Maria, aka mercenary Maria, officiated over the marina in long skirts that swept the pier as she raked in dinero, pesos, and dollars.

Marina de La Paz was spiffy, with a restaurant and bar overlooking the water and a hundred boats. Facilities included three showers with squeaky clean toilets and an air-conditioned office, painted a tasteful gray and mauve, offering fax, phone, and copying services. This was all Maria's work. Her milquetoast husband always hovered in the background.

The centerpiece of the marina was Club Cruceros, open 24/7, where notices were posted for cruisers. The club offered a book and magazine exchange, and a depository for cruisers to receive mail and parts. It contained the community VHF radio, always busy with conversations to and from the fleet, and a telephone for international calls with direct access to the AT&T operator, who accepted credit cards and collect calls. The telephone office downtown, the Larga Distancia, charged two bucks to place a collect call. And then only for the first five minutes.

Most cruisers used Ham or SSB radio, or faxes to relay personal or business messages. Everyone monitored channel 22 on VHF and listened to the La Paz area cruisers' net every morning at 8 a.m. except Sundays. Slip prices were less than half that of the Cabo marina so I signed up for six days, wincing as I handed over $107, including the key deposit. Even at half the Cabo tariff, I couldn't afford to stay long, and would soon have to anchor out.

Terry, self-named *the professional idiot*, was a skinny toothpick of fifty with a bushy mustache and hair like a fuller brush. He was mostly into beer and his video camera. He'd sailed *Eye of Infinity*, a fifteen-foot boat, from Monterrey to La Paz and made other improbable voyages in his tiny boat, including to Tokyo. But he'd freaked out during the trip down to La Paz and was building a trailer to tote *Eye of Infinity* back to the States. There he would prepare to sail her to Hawaii by painting an eye on her bow, in an eight lying on its side. At The Dock, I bought Terry a beer and listened to his story while trying to keep from passing out with exhaustion. I inhaled my beer like chilled nectar, intoxicated by the smell of French fries. Then I waved at Terry and staggered off to take a shower, collapsing on the boat. But I was too tired to sleep.

Perhaps I could repair everything for a lot more money than I had. Maria told me to listen to the morning net, where I'd find help with my broken boom and toasted engine. The Cruiser's net followed the same format every day, lasting fifteen to twenty-five minutes with volunteer cruisers taking weekly turns to host net control. The first announcement told everyone to turn their radios to high power, pushing coverage from El Centenario, ten miles south of La Paz, to Pichilinque, the ferry terminal five miles north of town where ferries sailed for Mazatlán.

The first call-out was for emergencies, priority, and medical traffic. During the weeks I tuned in, this included a cruiser bitten on the butt by a brown recluse spider, which had gone undiagnosed for two weeks. He needed blood donations, or he'd die of gangrene. This was a few years before everyone was on the internet. Cruiser Ham operators, which included me, relayed messages from the States, Canada, Australia, and Germany, the primary origins of the La Paz cruising community.

The net read the satellite weather forecast and the moderator described hurricanes forming in the zone of convection, zero to ten degrees north latitude. During my second week in La Paz, Hurricane Calvin headed our way, causing unending consternation because half the fleet had swallowed the anchor and would never leave, or perhaps ever sail again--even to avoid a hurricane.

Calcification had set in. Many had homes ashore, several where the wife spent her time, leaving the husband on the boat. The hurricane missed the anchorage by thirty miles, downgraded it to a tropical depression, producing only light sprinkles but tons of destructive wind.

Miss Canada was captained by a sixty-year-old single-hander anchored out on a large trimaran, and she always read the weather, putting the fleet to sleep: "Forrrrr Tueeesdaaay, Auguuuust fiiiirst, at one hundred hoooours, tide two-point-ooooone feeeeeet."

Tides swept through the La Paz channel at three knots, enough to launch any lightly anchored boat to oblivion. When combined with howling Coromuel winds from the south, boats blew away, hence for those who could afford it, a universal preference for slips in the marina. Many more were anchored out, some in tidal currents next to the channel, a two-mile swath in front of downtown La Paz. Others anchored across the sandbar, next to El Mogote, where the cruiser had sat on the brown recluse spider. The sandbar was formed by a long and desolate ten-mile-long dune that bisected the huge Bahia de La Paz. The current was slack three or four times a day, lasting as long as an entire minute, and then the maelstrom would begin in the opposite direction. A beer can floating looked like it was water skiing.

The next net category was mail call based on the name of the boat instead of the folks aboard. This was a typical list: "Adventure, Beto, Carioca III, Elaine, Endeavor, Free Run, Grendel, Holly Ann, Indulgence, Jedidiah, Karefree, Lubeck, Marikai, Nomad, Oceanus, Periplus, Quasar, Redwings, Simplicity, T'n Honey, and Zorba. Always alphabetical.

Net control asked those going to the States to identify themselves if they were kindly willing to carry letters from the fleet to mail stateside. Mexican postage cost twice that of U.S. postage, and letters mailed in Mexico took three or four times longer to deliver statewide, assuming they arrived at all. Cruisers' mail with U.S. stamps could also catch one of the daily flights to Los Angeles or Tucson.

Every twenty-four hours, Marina de La Paz reported four or five boats receiving faxes. When I ordered parts from San Diego, I sent and received a fax every day, making *Grendel* a name familiar to the fleet. Two dollars to receive and five to send. Much cheaper and easier than the phone.

The net asked for new arrivals and departures, lost and found, those needing crew, or those wanting to crew. Not much action in these categories. Next came announcements, such as the Spanish club meeting at El Cortijo restaurant on Friday morning at 9 a.m. Or what was playing at the community opera on Friday. There were discussions of how to lure whales off the El Mogote sandbar, where they were unerringly intent on committing suicide.

Last came the two most active categories: help needed and trades wanted. A sailboat can be classified by the number of problems per mile sailed, multiplied by the length of the boat. Seemingly, every single boat was an accident waiting to happen, aggravated by saltwater, salt air, extreme humidity and heat, sea electricity that ate every kind of metal, and unfriendly natives. Complicated by the incompetency of their skippers. Hearing of dinghies lost, motors dropped or trashed, sails ripped, masts toppled, fires, and boats scuttled on rocks, I began feeling less like the Lone Ranger. This was our suburban life.

I came in on the *new arrivals* chunk of the net, and during "help needed." I asked for advice on repairing a broken boom. Someone advised me to call *Redwings*, and I did. Abe on *Redwings* rated a book of his own, an old salt who'd earned the name by the circles under his armpits. He was a curmudgeon deluxe,

62

a miniature Abe Lincoln down to his warts and scraggly beard, skinny with a hooked nose and hard, bony face, weighing a hundred pounds, max. He'd have been the spitting image of Honest Abe if Lincoln had been five-foot-three. And he hadn't bathed for weeks.

Abe's real name was George, but no one knew that. He became my companion and transportation around La Paz, a self-anointed jack and master of all trades and girl-chaser supreme, everyone's most unforgettable character. He drove a crumpled combination station wagon and pick-up that was the washed-out color of the Sonoran Desert, a Canadian with New Mexico license plates who'd never been to New Mexico.

My first meeting with Abe began on my first morning in La Paz, an hour after the net. He hurried over to *Grendel* after my plea for help, and I figured he smelled money, but his first words were a lecture. "Now, don't you go telling anyone that you're paying me. That's illegal down here. If they ask, say I'm telling you where to find stuff. Understand?" He stood smacking his lips, working his jaw, wearing a sizeable sombrero and a ragged shirt with shorts sagging over scrawny bones.

Yes, father, *sir*. The tone was unmistakable, but I needed too much help to care. He assigned me a list of chores, the first being to drain the oil and replace it with a heavier weight in the hope the engine would start. Voila, and the engine started right up with forty pounds of pressure. Abe only stuck around for ten minutes, telling me to unbolt the boom. He'd find a welder and a cylindrical strut to brace the break from the inside, playing Billy Goat Gruff, standing there with his hands on his hips, as skinny as fiber optic. He'd also find someone to straighten the Tillermaster shaft and locate an engine mechanic.

Abe had sailed down from Canada eight years before and claimed to know where to find anything in La Paz. He could get anything done that was doable, which often wasn't much. Abe had an opinion on everything, professing an intimate knowledge of La Paz and Mexican politics, local personalities, and hundreds of cruisers. According to Abe, most of the La Paz sailing community were ex-pat Americans who'd sailed this far and would venture no farther. Half were alcoholics.

The next day, Abe and I loaded the dinghy motor, Danforth anchor, and broken boom into his decrepit truck for delivery to a welder, assuming we could find one. The first repair worked out super, as he straightened the Tillermaster shaft for a measly ten pesos, $3.33 back then. We found a welder named Joe, a bantam rooster in an immaculate white shirt. After years in LA, Joe spoke perfect English, promising the boom and Danforth anchor would be ready by Monday. I hadn't a clue what day that was, but it sounded soon. When we checked back on Monday, Joe had done nothing because he had neither the equipment nor the skill to weld aluminum.

After the success of straightening the Tillermaster shaft, Abe took me to his

favorite restaurant for *la comida del dia*, the daily lunch special, a four-course meal for eight and a half pesos; i.e., $2.64. The day's special was a starter of soup chowder jammed with a half-pound of fish, half a barbecued chicken accompanied by the usual rice and beans, and flan for dessert. I bought lunch for Abe, paying six dollars with drinks. During months in La Paz, I ate at El Cortijo every single day.

I sat marveling at El Cortijo being such a deal, sitting on the balcony with other diners, watching mini-skirted Mexican sex pots parade below in skimpy skirts. Abe was the most attentive of all, and I might have been a close second. Abe had operated cranes, chased women, and supervised the sets and locations for *Five Easy Pieces*, according to Abe. But it rang true. The women part was without question. He chatted them up in every age group, size, and shape, and had become the godfather to the granddaughter of the El Cortijo restaurant family, a perpetual suitor of the waitresses, and gawker at every miniskirted, tight-panted, low-cut blouse within sight of the El Cortijo balcony.

Abe was excited, chortling with an insane cackle, "Did ya see that one?" He'd smack his lips, crack his jaw, and smirk, though I couldn't have missed "that one" since we were peering over the El Cortijo balcony together. This randy sixty-one-year-old billy goat had placed a seven-dollar want ad in the *La Paz* newspaper, trolling for local women. He received eighteen responses and in the next few weeks, met five women, regaling me with hours of detail after each date. If these women were as sexy and accommodating as Abe said, he'd have been too exhausted to work on *Grendel*. Every single lady was voluptuous, nubile, seductive, inviting, flirtatious, arousing, stimulating, slinky, provoking, provocative, and titillating. I met several of these misdescribed ladies, proving Abe's talent for gross exaggeration.

3

July 1993

I wrote friends in Phoenix and gave them my address, figuring it'd filter back to Mary. If I didn't hear from her in a week or two, I'd drop her a brief note, telling her I missed her, but I wouldn't get too sentimental, more like "Miss you, bitch." She might detect a certain hostility.

I checked the batteries, and the acid in every cell was down to the core. Another stroke of negligence. The list of chores accumulated: cleaning the boat, packing the radar to ship back to the States, tinkering with the dinghy motor, replacing a rudder bolt, convincing Abe to check whether they'd welded the boom, exploring why the bilge pump was acting up, and finding a dentist to clean my teeth. The major success story was getting the Danforth, the light anchor, welded for $6.67. Then I had to have it galvanized to protect the weld from seawater, which corrodes everything.

After a week, I received a box of magazines and three packets of first-class mail from friends and editors, the first in a month, including two incoherent letters from Mary. She said she missed me a lot but said nothing about *Grendel*, sailing, or living on the boat. To me, this omission made the letters meaningless. I wrote her back, pointing out what she failed to say. So, BFD. We had to face reality.

At El Cortijo, I tried improving my lamentable Spanish. Roberto, the waiter, would say, "*Como estas?*" and I'd stand there thinking about several courses of Spanish 101 I'd fumbled through. Then I'd mutter, "*Muy bien, gracias,*" *gringo* stamped across my forehead. I could only remember simple Spanish phrases in the present tense, never finding the time to study the vocabulary and verb declensions I'd heroically transcribed to a stack of flashcards.

Roberto wore a pert mustache like a Mexican TV host, with dark eyes and immaculate hair, dressed in white, bowing as he asked what I wanted for lunch. The *pescado*, of course, and to make conversation I added, "*y un cerveza, tambien.*" *Cerveza* was the first word I'd learned in Spanish, decades ago. This added fifty percent, $1.33 to the lunch bill, the first time I'd had a beer in two weeks. The El Cortijo management must have been ecstatic at the big-spending, eccentric *gringo* who showed up every day and after scarfing the daily special, spent an hour writing. The book I was working on was published twenty-five years later, titled *Scribes of the Tribe, The Great Thinkers on Religion and Ethics*.

Roberto poured the beer and I said, "*Muchas gracias.*" Fucking native, me. The *gringo* who liked more hot sauce and spices than the locals, scribbling on the balcony between glances at ladies parading and boats bobbing on the brilliant blue sea, a small portion of the La Paz fleet.

Mary left a phone message that she'd arrive at the La Paz airport on Friday, July 16, at 9:30 p.m. What a surprise. Did I want Mary in La Paz for a week? A woman named Patti was flying down from Denver to meet me on July 23, the day Mary would leave. Abe put it best: "Either feathers or too much chicken." OMG. It was remote that Patti would work out, like many women who'd contacted me about sailing: Lael, Pamela, Brenda, and Magdalena. They'd responded to a cryptic ad that ran once in *Latitude 38*, an inexpensive sailing magazine out of San Francisco. No one I corresponded with was compatible. Like I'm picky? Maybe. Though with the help I needed on the boat, being picky bordered on the absurd.

Mary had been my best relationship ever, lasting nine years, but that meant nothing if she was unable to leave her cushy stateside job, though I couldn't gripe at her logic. Anyone would be reluctant to retire at age forty-three to live on a boat manned by Captain Klutz.

Patti was forty-five, a slender, attractive blonde, and successful real estate broker who intended to retire in a few months. She claimed boat skills and said she was a hard worker, positive, and patient. Mary was a hard worker, but was often pessimistic and almost always impatient. I found it interesting that Patti said she "hadn't always made the best choices" but "took instruction well." Whips and chains came to mind.

La Paz's near-miss hurricane hit the fleet with forty-five-knot winds, creating raucous times for cruisers trying to keep their boats from blowing onto the docks--or for those anchored out, from blowing away and grounding. To celebrate surviving the hurricane, Abe suggested a night out at El Ranchito and El Rey, nightclubs with nocturnal *especiales* ten miles south of town. I agreed because I wanted to check out the weird atmosphere Abe described, and the taco special he raved about. What a night.

El Ranchito and El Rey lit the desert for miles, sitting next to each other in a rectangular compound, and we were the only *gringos*. Each bar featured two dozen women, of which three were attractive at El Ranchito and one passable at El Rey. Abe had timed our arrival for the midnight show at El Ranchito, which, before the women took the stage, opened with an agonizing male singer. The first chubby dancer took four songs to disrobe, and we voted unanimously that it would have been a far, far better thing if she hadn't bothered.

Though the show was boring, the interior, women, and clientele were fascinating. The club was large, featuring a thirty-five-foot stage tiled in black and white with an ample dance floor. The waiters wore white shoes, tuxedo shirts with black bow ties, and orange paper hats, shifty bastards who short-changed customers, doing very well fleecing inebriated locals. Girls hustled dances for five pesos ($1.67 each), drinks five dollars, and a backroom for fifty dollars. The locals favored the less attractive women, those in scanty bulgy costumes. Almost all were comically overweight while the few slender lovelies sat on the sidelines, unnoticed.

El Ranchito was full, a hundred guys at twenty-five tables, many belligerently drunk. The three attractive women took a crack at Abe and me. When I walked in the door, one asked me to dance. I said "No!", though she was nice looking in white shorts and loose black bustier

69

displaying soft luscious nestlings. I can't dance worth a damn and in any event, wasn't interested in female company.

The second attractive, slender woman wore a short white dress and asked Abe if I'd dance with her. She was the best-looking woman in the place, but I declined. I was not only broke, but besides being a terrible dancer, I was way too cheap to pay for a dance. The only other attractive lady sat in the booth next to us all night long, never making a move on anyone. The lovely lady in the white dress plopped down at our table between dances and Abe tried to chat her up while she and I studiously ignored each other

El Rey was tackier, but the beer was better and less expensive at $1.67 instead of the two dollars at El Ranchito. The only attractive lady wore tiny hot pants and a halter top. Soon after we arrived, the cops traipsed through the brothel. According to Abe, they were looking for *mordida*, free drinks, and their choice of a babe in the back room. The best deal was the dollar beef tacos sprinkled with fresh onion, tomato, and jalapenos. After scarfing two, it took half an hour to recover. Yummy hot.

The next afternoon, cruisers and locals went wild when twenty juvenile whales grounded in the bay on the El Mogote sand bar. I joined cruisers swimming out to help the whales off the sandbar, but it was hopeless. I could only look a whale in the eye as it responded with clicks. A massive powerboat lassoed each whale and tried to tow it to safety. Three times before sunset, the whales turned around after they'd been freed, re-grounding on the sandbar. The next morning, the whales had escaped on their own.

Three weeks after arrival in La Paz, I'd made no progress on welding or replacing the boom. I gave up on welding because no one had the expertise or tools to repair aluminum. Other cruisers suggested I contact a marine service in California, most efficiently accomplished by fax, which was prohibitively expensive, five dollars to send one page and two dollars to receive, though less expensive than phone calls, which were worse. After waiting an hour for an operator and an open line, they cost three dollars a minute. I'd sent a dozen faxes and still made no progress on finding a replacement boom until finally, a marine service faxed me, saying it'd found a replacement. So, I ordered the new boom and tried to figure out how to avoid Mexico City customs and get it down to La Paz without delay.

Mexico's poverty was depressing. According to *The Mexico City News*, an English-language newspaper, 91.9 percent of Mexicans were unable to afford necessities. No wonder they despised *gringos* and our apparent wealth, no matter how poor we thought we were. In 1993, except for fresh fruit and vegetables, Mexico imported most things from the States, doubling prices to twice that of the U.S. Mexican schools taught kids the United States had stolen California, Texas, New Mexico, and Arizona, and Mexico deserved that land back. Hundreds of years of resentment had built up between the two countries, such as on the U.S. side with "*Remember the Alamo.*"

I hadn't seen Mary for six months and almost didn't recognize her when Abe drove me to the airport. This was crazy because she'd only cut her hair. Her fabulous legs and sleek weight-lifting physique were unchanged. Abe rushed us back to the boat, where we fell into the king-sized forepeak bunk for hours of physicality. We began the week in a familiar domestic routine, her reading and me writing, going for a run before breakfast, lunch at El Cortijo, and walking around La Paz, soon tiring of both La Paz and Abe. So, we sailed up the Sea of Cortez.

Backing out of the slip, I was at my klutziest. Mary had to be screaming inside when I almost tore the dinghy off the davits and nosed into the dock, where fellow cruisers fended me off. When we were finally underway, I was shaking. Mary couldn't have missed my latest example of ineptitude. No one would want to sail with me. It was too much work, impossible to keep me out of trouble.

I loosened the huge spinnaker, and we sailed proudly out of the harbor until I glanced at the gauges. The oil pressure had dropped to thirteen instead of the optimal forty-five, which registered on my poor brain at the exact moment when I needed to tack the genoa. Even with Mary pulling, puffing, and bitching, the genoa refused to slide over the staysail.

I ran down below and checked the oil pressure, but in all the panic, I failed to replace the dipstick for a chaotic twenty minutes, resulting in oil spewing all over the engine compartment. The engine refused to rev above 1300 RPMs, so we crept along leisurely, like a snail, taking three hours of put-put-putting to cover five miles to the secluded bay I'd selected.

At sunset, we dropped anchor in isolated Caleta Lobos, and tensions dissolved. The atmosphere transformed to idyllic and we took deck showers, chased with fresh salsa, guacamole, and chips and Mary proclaimed the fiery red sunset gorgeous. We sipped cocktails until the stars came out, doing little or nothing for the next four days, making up for missed carnality before sailing back to La Paz, where I introduced Mary to cruising friends.

I still hadn't a clue whether she might join me on the boat but I wasn't going to push her, doubting she would, putting the odds at fifty-fifty. She hesitated because she said: 1) she was too impatient and couldn't handle the *mañana*-culture in Mexico, or another month in La Paz, though we had no idea it'd take a hell of a lot longer than a month to get *Grendel* ready for long-distance sailing. And 2) I tried to control her. I didn't know what that meant, but mum was the word. We agreed on the two most important things to us: travel and tons of wild and crazy lovemaking.

I introduced Mary to the cruisers, who not only loved her but were enamored, from Joe on *Endeavor* to Lourdes and Pete on *Holly Ann*, and everyone else she met. Mary and I had a "Last Supper" at a fancy downtown restaurant. She had little tolerance for alcohol and was looped on a single order of two-for-one margaritas. I helped her walk next door to Caffe Venezia for Italian ice cream, before retiring to the boat for a "Last Meditation." It'd take a week to recover physically. Mentally, who knew?

The next morning, we attended weekly Spanish class at the marina restaurant with a dozen other cruisers and picked up mail for Mary to drop stateside. Joe, a former fighter pilot, and I had become firm friends. We took Mary to the airport, where Mary and I kissed and hugged goodbye. She tried to avoid crying and succeeded. I was too numb to cry. Patti flew in that afternoon.

4

August 1993

Patti was lovely, knowledgeable, broadly traveled, and independent, supporting herself. She seemed to like me. Or at least said she had a great time, but *Grendel* was way too small for her. She hated coming below, preferring to stay on deck in the open air. Patti seemed to know everything from cooking and carpentry to electrical and mechanic arts. She'd traveled the world, living in Austria for a year and learning German, living in Spain for a few months, and spending time on Socorro Island, where she'd ridden giant manta rays. I was most impressed by how Patti absorbed everything around her, paying attention to the details of everything. She looked up every Spanish word she didn't know and closely examined flowers, rocks, cactus, seashells, plants, bushes, fossils...stuff no one else would notice. I missed Mary.

Patti was looking for a boat with a substantial galley to prepare sumptuous meals, which eliminated *Grendel,* a mere thirty-five-footer. When we got back to La Paz after three days anchored out, I received a three-page letter from Mary. I wrote Mary back and gave the letter to Patti to mail stateside. My cruising cronies opined that although Patti was a cutey, Mary was a far better choice, but I knew that. Taking Patti back to the airport was a joy. After two hectic weeks, I craved not having to entertain anyone, anymore, maybe ever.

Abe invited me to his boat, a classic Bristol Channel Cutter, a fabulous boat disguised by terminal hoarding. He'd stacked the boat with rubbish, inside and out. What a dump. Piles of rusty chain littered the bow, junk covered every surface, and the whole place smelled as musty as the underside of a wet tarp. The only tidy spot was a narrow bunk in the main salon that doubled as a couch, where he pursued his hound-dog seduction scenarios. I guessed Abe hadn't cleaned the boat during its eight years in La Paz, or more likely, since it was launched.

I listened to an hour of Abe's blow-by-blow account of his latest date with ad responder Tammy. Abe, the smooth operator, had seduced her with beer and hot French kisses until, in Abe's words, "She was about to explode like a pressure cooker." I choked back laughter. Any woman kissing Abe showed an uncommon lack of taste. His only appeal was who he wasn't. He wasn't a macho Mexican man who Mexican women uniformly reported being deathly sick of. Ninety-nine percent of the Mexican male population, according to Abe's ad-responders, treated women like dirt, preferring their women in the kitchen, barefoot and pregnant, forbidden to speak unless told what to say.

Things got so hot with Tammy that Abe missed a 5 p.m. date with Sara, a twenty-year-old hottie he'd been out with once, likely hot only in Abe's overheated imagination. Abe described the two dates in excruciating detail, both ladies a little plump, but hey. Abe disliked Sara because she had class, which offended Abe, who had no class at all. The florid description of his two dates took two hours, intertwined with hilarious descriptions ranging from strategic moles to sweat trickling between humongous breasts, amusing tales of fondling jugs, sticky fingers, and throat tonguing. He bragged about juggling three babes at once, though he couldn't have lifted a single one off the floor.

Maria put my name on the waiting list for a long-term slip, which was inexpensive after I anchored out, unable to afford the daily rate for a marina slip. Then the oarlock on the dinghy broke, so I was unable to row to shore from the anchorage. I mentioned my dinghy dilemma to my cruising pals and was flabbergasted at their kindness. Pete on *Holly Ann* gave me a horseshoe and pin to weld onto the oarlock, and Joe on *Endeavor* insisted I borrow his big rubber dinghy and outboard motor until I found a welder. Compared to my dinghy, Joe's was not only stable but the big outboard would get me to shore in seconds. I gratefully accepted Joe's loan, which saved me from rowing half a mile to shore. But I spent a sleepless first night worrying about the expensive dinghy and motor bobbing behind *Grendel*, afraid it'd either come untied or someone would steal it. I could imagine a half dozen catastrophes that would make me obligated to buy a new dingy and outboard motor for Joe.

My new boom arrived in San Diego, so I had to find a cruiser to deliver it to La Paz. The usual pay for this kind of favor was a fancy meal, drinks, and many heartfelt thanks, making me think I might get out of La Paz by the end of August. My usual pipe dream.

The oil pressure remained catastrophically low, so Abe corralled a motor mechanic named Pablo to take a look at the engine. I started it up, and they spent an hour discussing the engine's shortcomings in

76

Spanish. They thought Bardol, thick as honey and heavier than oil, might do the trick. Of course, it didn't. Final verdict: I'd trashed the engine. It was worthless, and I couldn't afford to replace it. This happened right after I received a six-page letter from Mary saying she might come live on the boat. What would she think of this mess? I could only use the engine in emergencies, and then it was virtually worthless. I was exhausted, trying to find parts and avoid interminable Mexican bureaucracy while waiting for hand-deliveries from the States.

I told Mary to decide by October 1 whether she would move onto the boat. On August 10, I received two letters from Mary, one dated July 1, stating she was ready to drop everything and move aboard. But the letter dated August 2 left me depressed and certain she wasn't coming. She was having problems with her son, a legitimate concern, and other reasons I considered excuses, ranging from her impatience to my dream of circumnavigation overshadowing her druthers, which she still failed to describe. Mary must have understood she was essential to the goal we'd worked toward for almost a decade but must have thought I wouldn't leave without her, not realizing that in my mind I'd left years before. If she wasn't coming on board, I had to get over her. We'd have to stop writing and leading each other on, and I would have to find someone else, either platonic, to help on the boat, or cozier. But I was so lazy. My head felt frozen, trying not to think about Mary, but that didn't work and I couldn't keep from crying. Too much pain for both of us.

Abe regaled me with apocryphal tales of seduction and sticky fingers with Tima, an outstanding example of womanhood, meaning Tammy was history. Abe reported vivid memories of substantial black nipples and offers of marriage. Best of all, Tima owned a beauty salon and could support Abe in the style to which he'd dearly like to become accustomed.

I loaned Abe a copy of my first book, *Myths of the Tribe*, published two months before by Prometheus Books in New York. He was gaga over it, fascinated with the checkered history of our many religions and their disconnect from morality, saying, "It condenses everything you know but haven't thought of yet."

I was ecstatic when Kinko offered to ship my boom to La Paz for fifty dollars. It'd take a week because sections of the Baja Road had been washed out and closed by the recent hurricane. Abe was irate I'd consider paying fifty dollars to Kinko for a scheduled delivery run, but I was damn tired of being stuck in La Paz, and other cruisers urged me to take the offer. I also received two faxes from Mary, telling me to call her collect. I did, and she said she was seventy-five percent certain she'd come live on the boat. Whipsaw, whiplash. She liked my letters, replete with stories featuring her in steamy situations. Anyway, that was my theory.

A few days later, Kinko said it couldn't ship the boom to La Paz because parts of the Baja Road were still washed out. So, after waiting a month, I had no choice but to head up to the States to retrieve the damn boom. Oh, and attend my oldest daughter's wedding in Wisconsin. I found a ride to Phoenix, leaving two days later on September 1. Then disaster struck. Joe's dinghy and motor disappeared. It had been bobbing behind *Grendel* at 3 a.m., gone at 6.

I announced the dinghy's absence on cruiser radio channel 22. "Attention, fleet. If anyone has seen a dinghy, hard bottom inflatable with an Evinrude ten-horse outboard, lost between 3 a.m. and 6 a.m., please come back to *Grendel*."

Dead silence in response. I wandered around the boat in shock, doing my daily routine in a daze. Several friends searched for the dinghy while Abe and I spent four hours combing sixteen miles of beach where he figured the dinghy might have drifted on the tide between 3 a.m. and 6. I knew I'd tied the dinghy off the stern improperly. Knots were my biggest weakness, along with mechanical and electrical incompetency, and a lamentable lack of common sense. As Abe and I returned to La Paz, *Holly Ann* called and said the dinghy had been recovered at the La Paz Naval Base.

The naval base was an adventure, remarkably spotless amid garbage-strewn Mexico, where Abe and I found the dashing female officers exceptionally kind and helpful. I spent an hour signing reams of paper necessary to spring the wayward dinghy. Abe's assistance in combing the beaches earned him a splash-out dinner at an air-conditioned restaurant, where I dropped twelve bucks.

5

September 1993

I'd packed for the eight hundred-mile drive to San Diego when the driver called and said his starter was kaput, postponing our trip for twenty-four hours. Good thing, because I got a fax from Mary saying she was quitting her job as head of the accounting department at the largest private construction firm in Arizona, and I should call her. On the phone, she said she had to stay in Phoenix to train her replacement until December 1. Her boss was a reasonable guy who was about to retire and buy a boat. He was freaked out she was quitting, offering $5,000 in moving expenses to stay until December. Mary was still worried. What if she didn't like sailing after a few months? What if she couldn't stand being on the boat? I pointed out we'd had great fun on over a dozen sailing charters all over the world, from Belize to Greece, and suggested we discuss it later. What could I say? She was afraid she didn't have enough money saved to get rid of most of her earthly possessions and leave a cushy job. We hung up, saying, "Love you madly."

I left before with Charlie 6 a.m. to begin the drive to San Diego, carrying a wish list for my cruising buddies, items to tote back down. For example, Abe wanted a Spanish-English dictionary and a ton of Fixodent for his dentures. Charlie and I made it halfway to San Diego, to Guerrero

Negro by 4:30 p.m. We split a motel room for thirty-one dollars, fuel for sixty, and ate dinner for seven. The next day we got to San Diego at 6 p.m. and I bought a fifty-nine dollar standby plane ticket to Phoenix, leaving at 8 p.m. Mary met me at the airport at 9 p.m., so hyper she couldn't sleep. The next day, we went shopping for topsiders, shorts, and folding bikes. My biggest impression was the lack of garbage on the streets.

Out of nowhere, though we'd never before thought it necessary or advisable, Mary and I decided to get married. Mary worried about living together in conservative countries, especially Muslim ones. The idea felt strange since we'd both been burned before, and the next day, Mary changed her mind, deciding we shouldn't get married. Instead, we should fake a marriage certificate to bandy about as needed. So much for a long engagement.

We decided on a fake wedding celebration, making frivolous decisions willy-nilly. The marriage announcement thrilled our friends, but they were shocked at our blasé attitude. We had fun putting together a guest list of a dozen closest friends that quickly expanded to two dozen, and ended up chickening out of a fake wedding. I asked a former law school student of mine, who'd become a judge, to perform the ceremony in his chambers.

We almost forgot to get a license, grabbing it on the way to Judge Wiehn's office. On arrival, we'd forgotten to buy rings. John Wiehn knew me too well, anticipating our cavalier attitudes, providing a nautical ceremony with colorful cloth bracelets woven by his niece. Mary and I were almost in contempt of court, stifling laughter at John's

81

solemn officiating. Afterward, he confided that for two years my second wife's best friend had been sleeping with the judge's best friend, illustrating the close-knit legal community in Phoenix. So, we invited my second ex-wife's best friend and the judge's best friend to our wedding reception on Sunday.

The reception was a festive party with Mary's extended Greek family and sixteen of our friends, resulting in a modest harvest of cash toward our sailing venture. I presented copies of my newly published book to several attendees. Huge thrill, I'm sure.

A week later, Mary suffered buyer's remorse, complaining I was controlling her, but never explaining exactly how. She was fine, and then she wasn't. I had to fly to Chicago to attend the third wedding of Tania, my oldest daughter. My absence would give Mary a chance to relax and decide what she wanted to do. I told her if she had second thoughts we could go our separate ways, but that would be the end.

Tania and Richard, her fiancé, picked me up at Chicago Midway Airport for the drive to Manitowoc, Wisconsin. It took two and a half hours in bad traffic. I was horrified, realizing how much trouble they'd gone to, picking me up in Chicago, taking a day off work, and cutting a day off the time they had available for wedding preparations.

I babysat Tania's kids. Nine-year-old Ashley, my oldest granddaughter, rattled off her spelling words perfectly, and I was impressed. They rewarded my babysitting with a family dinner, inviting my ex-wife Kay and former mother-in-law Jane, who were flabbergasted by my cheerful civility. I was pretty impressed too. Tania diplomatically sat between me and her mom and grandmother.

I stayed at Tania and Richards house where they spent the bulk of their time during the week before the wedding yelling at each other, making it difficult to understand why they wanted to get married in the first place. I was sure it wouldn't last. It was so bad I moved out and stayed at a motel that cost thirty-four dollars a night, a fortune on my meager sailing budget.

As I was leaving to take Richard and his entourage to the wedding, Tania showed up at my motel room. She asked if she was presentable, hair up in a freshly colored red bun. I was diplomatic and said she looked fine, a frazzled dumpling with chubby cheeks. Considerable Wisconsin food was deep-fried, from cheese curds to bratwurst and butter cakes, and drinking beer was the hands-down favorite pastime. Obesity seemed to be an occupational hazard of living in Wisconsin.

When Tania left, I went to pick up the groom and his four best men, making sure they got to the wedding on time. They were drinking beer and couldn't understand why I was wearing a tux. I reminded them the wedding began in half an hour, which sent them into an inebriated panic. They scurried around, flustered and hilarious to watch. We arrived five minutes late, straggling into the church to find a restive audience.

My ex-wife Kay gave away the bride. I had no role because I didn't know until the last minute whether I could attend. But the bride and groom asked me to take wedding photos, which I'd done at Tania's second and last wedding in 1981 at Fort Carson Army Base in Colorado. Kay, like Tania, was many pounds overweight. Tania explained her weight as being four and a half months pregnant. I assumed Tania and Richard wouldn't have otherwise gotten married.

Jane, my ex-mother-in-law, asked me, the heretic, to read I Corinthians 13 on love. I had the grace to agree, doing my best Charlton Heston imitation, glowing with goodwill, sitting between Jane and Kay at the wedding. Taking photos of the wedding and attendees gave me hours of splendid fun, and I took another two hundred photos at the reception, which cost $15,000. Whoa, $15,000 back then was $28,000 in 2021, more than my yearly budget after paying child support to my second wife on behalf of my third child. I danced with Tania's boss's girlfriend and, perhaps because I can't dance, accidentally nudged her left breast. I said I hadn't touched her, and she said I had. I said it probably felt pretty dang terrific, and she agreed. Wisconsin wedding parties are beyond jovial.

I gave the newlyweds a copy of my newly published book with a hundred-dollar bill tucked inside, curious whether they'd ever find the money. Thirty years later, I still haven't a clue. Bad dad. The marriage lasted ten years, nine years longer than I guessed it would. Inertia can do wonders for a marriage.

I insisted on flying back to Chicago from Milwaukee, taking a scenic puddle jumper along the shoreline of Lake Michigan to Midway Airport, feeling nostalgic when the plane wheeled over the University of Chicago, my law school alma mater. Tania and Richard had given me a fancy shot glass with a pewter crest that said "Dave and Mary, 9-9-93," which made me miss Mary. I'd beaten Tania to wedding number three by a mere two weeks.

84

Mary was waiting at the curb when I shot out of the Phoenix airport, wearing a full skirt, reminiscent of the fatal attraction about which Mary has advised me to say nothing further. I considered it a superb homecoming, ending in our favorite game of slave poker, which we both won, always.

Abe sent a fax saying the boom had arrived in La Paz a week ago. I owed someone big-time for bringing it down, but who? I bought polarized blue-blocker sunglasses for Abe along with the other stuff he wanted, and new fold-up bikes for Mary and me. On the last day of September, I drove to San Diego in a U-Haul truck, stuffed to the gills with Mary's stuff, waiting for Joe on *Endeavor* to show up to give me a ride back to La Paz.

6

October 1993

My first stop in San Diego was at West Marine, where I picked up miscellany for *Grendel*: a 7/16 inch bolt, sailing gloves, cockpit plug, and batteries for the Walkman. In Cardiff by the Sea, I visited Marty, who'd help install *Grendel*'s electronics in San Diego and Ensenada. Though otherwise intelligent, Marty had suffered brain damage in a dirt-bike accident and become a hoarder. At least, that was his excuse. He'd stacked his garage to the ceiling with worthless TVs, computers, lawnmowers, tires, and just plain junk. He always claimed to have what I needed, though there was no way of finding it, similar to the inside of his house. I congratulated Vickie, his latest chain-smoker girlfriend, for forging a trail through the dining room, so we could fetch beer from the kitchen. Vickie had packed the backyard with an almost impenetrable jungle of plants. They were a pair meant for each other.

I told Vickie she should "chuck out all the junk," and Marty said he'd kill her if she did. I threw stuff on top of other stuff to clear enough space around Marty's couch to fold the bed out for the night, waiting for Joe to show up in San Diego. Joe postponed his trip twice, and I ended up spending five clutter-filled party days at Marty's house.

When Joe finally showed up, we transferred Mary's stuff to the trunk and back seat of Joe's car and left for La Paz. Joe drank four *caguamas* of beer on the way to Guerrero Negro, the halfway point. When we arrived at 11 p.m., Joe stopped a *federale* to buy pot, swearing Mexican cops were the best and safest drug dealers in Mexico. Local and national governments paid cops far less than a living wage. The only way they could support their families was by soliciting bribes and dealing drugs.

Joe did all the driving, and we topped the long hill overlooking La Paz at 7 p.m. The vast circular bay lay below us, one of the best-protected in the world. The long club-footed peninsula of El Mogote formed the bay, providing 350 degrees of protection, and the sight made me feel like I was coming home.

The next morning, Abe sailed his dinghy to the dock as Joe and I unloaded Mary's stuff. Months before, while helping Joe pull another dinghy onto the dock, Abe had accidentally fallen in, ruining Abe's expensive handheld radio. Joe and Abe had argued for months over whether Joe was obligated to replace Abe's $500 radio, though Joe had little money and Abe had less. I stood with an armload of Mary's belongings, caught in the sniping between Joe and Abe, exasperated, asking whether I was required to choose sides and weapons. They laughed, but it wasn't pretty laughter. Me being super friendly to both drove them nuts, which was highly satisfying to me. In addition, there was a mix-up over video cassette movies Joe and Abe had loaned each other, and that never got sorted either.

I planned six projects my first day back, starting like gangbusters, forgetting I was back on Mexico time and lucky to finish one project a day. For one example, I borrowed a dozen charts to copy, covering the long Mexican coast. The only copy store in town could only duplicate half of a large chart at one time, and the process took hours. Then I had to cut and tape them together, filling a very long day.

Without bursting *Grendel* at the seams, I hadn't a clue how to get Mary's clothes and tons of books packed inside. When I still had two boxes of clothes and one box of books to stow, every compartment was full with no place left to put anything else. I repacked seven forepeak lockers, which took six hours, discarding three pillows, forty T-shirts, selected pots and pans, and a sweater. Abe promised to distribute this treasure trove to whoever wanted it. For all I cared, he could sell it and pocket the proceeds.

Abe and I worked all day, trying to install the new boom, but it wouldn't fit. I'd have to return it. Damn, damn, damn, a four-month-long problem no closer to a solution. I'd have to find a way to transport the new boom back to San Diego and locate the proper-sized boom, assuming such an animal existed. Abe suggested altering the boom at the abandoned Pepsi plant north of town, recently converted to a machine shop and welding center. For a measly forty dollars, the welding center said it could weld the gooseneck and cut a slit to rig the boom. Based on previous experience, I figured this wouldn't work because Mexico had always dashed my hopes, without exception, so I discounted everything promised by anyone. But, because it'd take months to find the proper boom and ship it to Mexico, we gave the welding center a try. Abe and I loaded the sixteen-foot boom on the top of his truck, sticking off both ends, and optimistically drove to the Pepsi plant.

I was miserable without Mary and exhausted by the interminable waiting. My only consolation was writing. I worked on *Scribes*--an analysis of quotes by our greatest thinkers about the relationship between religions and morality. Not exactly popular fiction, or nonfiction for that matter.

When I visited Joe's boat, he introduced me to a lady named Lynn. Her first words were whether I knew Dave on *Grendel* because she'd heard he was looking for crew. That was enough for us to hit it right off. Lynn would be available the first week in November and might be able to deliver *Grendel* to San Diego, if necessary. With the wind almost always right on the nose, sailing up the Baja was one of the toughest stretches of ocean on the planet. Without having to refuel and relying on sails alone would require weeks of sailing a triangle, hundreds of miles offshore, before tacking back towards San Diego. The alternative was motoring into high waves for at two weeks and *Grendel's* motor was fit only for calm seas.

My list of boat repairs included the transmission linkage along with installing water filters, a mooring snubber, a dinghy-cable sleeve, a starter solenoid, and a mounting for the ham radio and tuner. Plus, I needed to deep-clean the inside of the boat. *Grendel* was pure white and showed every little smudge. I also needed to do laundry, replace a pump diaphragm, clean the outside of the boat, refill the propane, fix the manual water pump, touch up the teak, and clean the bottom. The list would take weeks and the outboard motor's carburetor still needed welding. Sailing around the world wasn't a leisurely proposition, ending with many who'd who'd arrived at their final destination in La Paz. These included *Barbinegras*, *The Rock*, *El Cheff*, and *La Chanote*, among many.

During a get-together with cruising chums, Joe announced his engagement to Patricia, a local lady who owned a sprawling ranch where Joe would become the new foreman. Joe and Patricia invited Mary and me to the wedding, and I told Mary about the planned festivities during an outrageously expensive ten-minute phone call made to plan our trip down the Mexican and Central American coasts. We were looking forward to Costa Rica, Acapulco, and Ixtapa-Zihuatanejo, not knowing we'd never visit on a sailboat. In 1998, we meandered around Mexico in an RV, taking a whole year to drive pretty much every road in the country, finding that Mexico is ginormous.

Joe's engagement-announcement party generated a heated argument between Joe and John, who lived in town and owned a small catamaran beached next to Joe's boat, *Endeavor*. John whiled away his days smoking pot and doing odd jobs for cruisers. The two almost came to blows, arguing whether the Mexican Navy or the *Federales* sold the best pot in La Paz. The party made it apparent that most cruisers detested Abe, who'd only work for those who hadn't disrespected him. Except for me. I always ragged Abe about his women and primitive backgammon skills.

Thanks to Abe and miracles of miracles, the Pepsi factory reworked the boom to fit. Henceforth, I would forgive Abe anything. We spent an afternoon drilling and riveting the newly altered boom, which meant Abe muttered, swore, and sweated, while I ran back and forth, serving ice-cold beers. The job took seven hours, rewarded by pitchers of more beer at El Molino, where we watched Toronto win the World Series. I paid Abe fifty dollars for his work on the boom, a bargain for both of us. My journal recorded: "Today I got no writing done. I know how to write but do not write, to speak but do not speak. I am a failure." Also, a dope.

Abe was my puppy dog, always underfoot, boring but helpful, cantankerous, and untidy. He left for Loreto with an off-the-wall scheme to renew his visa, and I hoped he'd have to stay at least a week. Best of all, Mary would arrive on December 1, a great relief because La Paz was boring me silly. The days were empty after Mary said she'd come live on the boat but hadn't yet arrived.

I dropped an irreplaceable bronze washer in the bilge, essential to operating the watermaker. It winked at me from deep in the corner of the bilge, but I couldn't reach it. The only three sources of washers in La Paz unanimously opined that crenelated washers did not exist in Mexico. I sat paralyzed, a pissant little washer keeping me from mutating seawater to fresh. Abe helped finish up three projects over the next three days, which meant he did the work while I served refreshments. Best of all, he somehow got the washer out of the bilge.

Abe also found an engine expert named Pablo to look at *Grendel*'s woebegone engine. Could we salvage it, or restore engine compression? Verdict, the engine needed a valve job. Cost, $83.33 to open the engine, pull and grind eight valves, reseat the valves, reassemble the engine, and give it a test run. Well worth it, assuming it worked. Of course, it didn't.

The cruisers threw a Halloween party at *Barbera Negras*, aka Blackbeard's, a downtown hotel. It featured a roasted pig with all the fixings, a live band, and unlimited booze. The cruisers wore costumes and quaffed dollar drinks, and most of the women were tipsy within the first hour. A lady named Star, a passable brunette I'd met once, came dressed as a slut in a mini-dress. She French-kissed me until I was able to push her away, which admittedly took some time. Jaime wore a robot outfit and Lisa came as a very sexy fly. Richard was an explorer, Kip and Jerry cavemen in skimpy leotards, Steve a flasher with a three-foot cock, Pam in a boob-pooching halter top, and a bandaged man, among many. Accompanied by deafening music.

Abe invited two women to the party and I couldn't imagine they'd show up, but they did: Catalina and Dora, both characters. Dora was tubby, accompanied by her one-year-old daughter, equally tubby. It miffed Catalina that Dora had brought her little girl because Abe had told Catalina the party was for adults only. Otherwise, Catalina would have brought her daughter. I spent four dollars on four drinks and was bored spitless, leaving by 9 p.m. Abe yelled at my disappearing back, "You party pooper." He reported staying until the party evaporated at 2 a.m.

7

November 1993

Pablo, my new engine mechanic, took two and a half hours to pull the pistons. He decided the engine needed too much work to repair because he couldn't tell whether the crankshaft and rods were sound. I called Marty in California to locate a new or used diesel engine to replace *Grendel*'s worthless *Atomic 4* gasoline engine. Without an engine, I couldn't leave La Paz.

I hosted my first cruiser's net, which took thirty-five minutes, setting a record for length. To the relief of the fleet, the second day went much faster, and I received accolades for efficiency. The highlight of the day was a DHL package from Mary with plane tickets from La Paz to Phoenix on November 20, returning on December 4. She wanted me to help her move onto the boat and was surprised I'd missed her so much. She was sure I'd want to dump her overboard after she'd been on board for a week or two. Hardly. Besides missing her, I desperately needed the help!

A week later, Mary offered to buy a new diesel engine for *Grendel*. I discussed the issue with Marty and also Morgan, who'd accompanied us on sailing trips to Greece and Belize with Morgan captaining the second Greek boat. He offered to carry a new engine down to La Paz on November 16 when he would be feather-bedding as crew on a vast yacht.

I told Mary to wait on buying a new diesel engine until Pablo decided how much it'd cost to fix the *Atomic 4*, perhaps as little as $500, versus $6,000 for a new engine. Another dumb decision, but I didn't want to be beholden, even to my wife. Plus, $6000 sounded like a lot of money. That was five months of my puny budget, and almost a year on Mary's. An emergency fund of $6000 sounded better than a new diesel engine.

Abe was feeling poorly, unable to help Pablo pull the engine, which took three hours. I corralled three guys to help carry the engine from the dock to the back of Pablo's pickup, which was exhausting. Then I found out that Abe had suffered a massive stroke.

A mutual friend of Abe's named Beto, who'd concocted the want-ad scheme to meet local women, took turns with me feeding Abe at the La Paz hospital. Abe couldn't feed himself, and Mexican hospitals provide no nursing care. If the family doesn't feed and bathe patients, they receive no care. Only cursory observation. The consulting neurosurgeon told me Abe's smoking three packs of cigarettes a day for twenty years had filled his carotid artery with nicotine residue, leaving scant space for blood flow. The stroke initially reduced Abe to a fuzzy life of diapers and drool, and a vocabulary of twenty-five words.

Two days later, I met at El Cortijo Restaurant with six other cruisers to decide Abe's future. Because he couldn't do anything for himself, the only question was when and how to ship him back to Canada. The stroke paralyzed Abe on the right side of his body, and he was barely conscious of those around him. It took two days for him to relearn how to drink from a glass. The first time I visited the hospital, Abe was lying in his excrement. Patients' families had to clean up the patients, and, of course, Abe had no family, except for the few cruisers who tolerated him. I mobilized the fleet to begin a fund to pay for Abe's necessaries, found diapers, and changed him. I also bought forty-nine dollars of medicine, which hospitals required families to provide. The only apparent purpose of a Mexican hospital was to allow patients to expire out of public view.

Beto and I asked the Canadian consul to evacuate Abe back to Canada, and he readily agreed. He knew Abe and liked him, but Abe said he'd rather die than return to Canada. It took days to pry the "why" out of Abe. Half the fleet speculated that Abe had outstanding criminal charges or child support arrearages. Come to find out, Abe hadn't talked to his daughter for years. Naturally, he was anxious about a surprise reunion with an estranged daughter when he was helpless and unable to take care of himself. So, I tried contacting Abe's daughter. No answer. The only phone number Abe had for his daughter was years out of date.

Someone broke into Abe's boat. Since the boat was a disaster area, I couldn't tell what had been taken. Ignoring a drawer emptied of music and movie tapes, the only missing item of value seemed to be a new handheld radio. In the meantime, Abe's health deteriorated. I tried to interest him in backgammon, but he no longer knew how to play. Abe wouldn't know the difference between Canada and Mexico, but if he ever recovered, he'd shoot me for helping send him back to Canada.

The vote on NAFTA was an important day in Mexico, marking a week of feeding Abe lunch, often helped by Beto. It took both of us to shower Abe, transferring him from the bed, washing him, and putting him back in bed. Yuck. What a relief when the Consul scheduled Abe's evacuation to Canada on Saturday. We'd auction off his stuff and send him the money. Except for proceeds from selling his boat, the proceeds wouldn't be much.

Pablo said it'd cost $1,500 for parts to fix the engine, which sounded like a lot less than $6,000, so after consulting with Morgan and Marty, I give Pablo the money. Mary was extremely upset that I hadn't let her buy a new diesel engine. She was certain replacement parts wouldn't improve the old gasping engine to like-new, and was equally pissed off at Morgan and Marty for recommending I buy parts instead of a new engine. Of course, she was right, though it took months to confirm.

At Beto's request, I went to the hospital to feed Abe and play a last game of backgammon. Abe was doing slightly better, able to move backgammon pieces correctly, but with no strategy in mind. When dinner came, Abe insisted on feeding himself. When I left, he cried and I felt terrible. Abe must have been thinking this was the last time he'd see me, though it was only the next-to-last time. He grabbed me and wouldn't let go, the same as in October when I returned from the States. I hugged him back, but he wouldn't stop crying. He knew the Consul had scheduled his evacuation to Canada the next morning.

Old Seadog rushed over before 6 a.m. and gave me a ride to the hospital. Beto had bathed and dressed Abe before I got there, so I shaved Abe, his last in Mexico. Then the hospital refused to let Abe leave without paying $1,800. I berated the hospital administrator and shamed him into reducing the bill to $300. To pay the balance, Beto and I arranged a loan from Club Cruceros, which was selling Abe's belongings at auction. The club took no risk because Abe's boat was worth at least $30,000, notwithstanding being filthy and crammed with junk. A Bristol Channel Cutter is a lovely boat, and Abe's could be cleaned up like new. After hours of bickering, the hospital released Abe to an ambulance, which Beto and I followed to the La Paz airport. We were two hours late for his scheduled flight, but the next plane to Vancouver left within the hour.

I waited with Abe in the back of the ambulance as Beto made last-minute arrangements with Aero México. The last time I saw Abe was when the ambulance crew carried his stretcher up the ramp. Abe couldn't see Beto and me wave goodbye, which ended a chapter in all our lives. Beto beat me to the airport lounge, where we chugged gin and tonics while watching Abe's plane depart. I tried visiting Abe when Mary and I RVed Vancouver Island in the 2000s, but Abe wasn't in the phone book and I'd forgotten his daughter's married name. Without Abe, I'd have never gotten the boat ready to go before Mary would arrive in December.

Morgan crewed to La Paz on a fancy yacht named *Marco Polo*, carrying down engine parts for *Grendel*. *Marco Polo* had rescued a disabled trimaran halfway down the Baja, delaying its arrival for two days. I stood on the dock when eighty-eight-foot *Marco Polo* berthed, impressively. Wow, a superyacht. Morgan was effusive, proffering my recently published book for an autograph. He introduced me to Captain

Uva, the captain's crazy, sexy girlfriend Andrea, engineer Dave, steward Carla, cook Gail, and handyman Carlos. My first assigned chore was finding a carton of cigarettes for Morgan and a case of beer for the crew. They unloaded my engine parts, and I delivered them to Pablo. The crew, Morgan, and I sat down for five hours of sea tales and bawdy drinking at *The Dock*, the marina bar and restaurant, during which the captain got into a nasty fight with his girlfriend and kicked her off the yacht.

Morgan and I sailing Grendel on San Diego Bay

The next morning, Morgan and I caught a ride to the airport. He flew home to LA, and I caught a puddle-jumper to Phoenix via Guaymas and Tucson, happy to meet Mary at the Phoenix airport. Thus began a hectic week of errands, finding boat parts, and lunching with relatives and old friends. We gave away tons of stuff we couldn't move on the boat, including Mary's professional working clothes, happily accepted by her three similarly-sized sisters.

8

December 1993

Mary's former employer threw her a raucous going-away dinner. She'd given up a substantial paycheck to move onto the boat, taking a risky early retirement. She'd also packed fifteen boxes to take to La Paz and I hadn't a clue how'd we'd cram their contents into an already over-stuffed *Grendel*. It'd cost $145 for each box to accompany us on the flight to La Paz, so we bought a thousand feet of stretch-wrap and bundled fifteen boxes into five huge parcels of seventy pounds each--the maximum allowed on a flight. Still expensive on a tight budget.

We had a tearful breakfast with Mary's parents, her three sisters, and their families. Two dozen people cried profusely, except for me. As we turned to leave, I asked Mary if she was still going, which turned crying into gurgling laughter. Of course, Mary's family considered us nuts. We were off-our-rockers, leaving lucrative jobs to go gallivanting around the world. They didn't understand that gallivanters were us, fulfilling a plan that took years. Mary's cold feet had been a mere hiccup.

Beto met us at the La Paz airport, then trucked us and our humongous boxes to *Grendel*, where Mary and I carried the boxes below and collapsed. We spent the next day unpacking and searching for places to stow things we'd have trouble ever finding again. We stacked every surface with Mary's belongings with nowhere to put them.

I counted it a miracle that the re-bored engine was back together and ready to go. Pablo came by to test the engine, but it wouldn't rev above a few hundred RPMs. I'd also installed a new refrigerator for $313, and it didn't work either. Ah, Mexico. But the refrigerator guy recharged the Freon, which fixed it. Phew. Too bad the engine wasn't as simple to repair, plaguing us to the end of our days on *Grendel*.

Pablo tried to realign the engine, spending six hours while eight other cruisers provided unending advice on exactly how Pablo should accomplish the task. Joe thought it was the cutlass bearing, so Pablo extracted the bearing, and it wasn't. Days wasted, along with hours of work. Other theories of what ailed the engine included the plugs, distributor, timing, and other maladies, all gobbledygook to me. After spending $2600 on engine parts and repairs, the engine remained useless.

After a long day of trouble-shooting, Pablo and his crew went AWOL. I went to Pablo's house and reminded him of our project. He showed up the next day with his crew and again removed the engine.

That night the *Endeavour* space shuttle orbited low over La Paz from SW to NE, wowing the populace at an organized watch party. We watched it at Beto's house, which he'd built himself, a shotgun series of rooms next to an enormous patio surrounded by two-story-high walls, wide enough for tables and chairs, which provided a superb platform for viewing the lights of La Paz as well as the space shuttle. Beto had successfully found a wife among the ladies who responded to the newspaper ad he and Abe had placed, and she was a superb cook, fixing wonderful meals during frequent visits by Mary and me.

After adjusting the carburetor for the nth time, the engine would rev to 2000 RPMs in reverse and 1600 forward, both less than adequate. We decided *Grendel* would never be ready to circumnavigate. In a scant two weeks sailing from Ensenada, I'd trashed too many major components. The most important component, the engine, seemed to be beyond repair.

By mid-December, Mary was ready to leave La Paz. I'd been hoping to leave for months, and told her we were danged near ready, always the incurable optimist. Beto casually observed that I seemed to be a little light on cruising knowledge, which was an understatement. My greatest concern was having no time to write, always interrupted by unending repairs and maintenance. Seamanship ranked among the least of my priorities.

Mary and I were both klutzes. We rode our bikes to Pemex for gasoline, and on the way back, Mary crashed her bike and skinned her knee. Once back on the boat, I spilled gasoline in the cockpit. Even after an hour of scrubbing, the overpowering smell was impossible to entirely erase. Our only break was the annual Christmas parade of boats decked with lights. We kept setting a date to leave La Paz and missed it every time, losing an entire day trying to fit the fold-up bikes on deck under the dinghy, and I still had no time for writing.

The next day we put the dinghy back on its stern davits and lashed the bikes to the deck, along with extra gas cans. At least I'd remembered to top up the reserve fuel. We thought we were ready to sail to Mazatlán,

102

but it began blowing hard and raining in sheets. It stayed nasty until Christmas Day, which we spent fixing a flat bike tire, replacing a membrane in the watermaker, and helping a fellow cruiser repair a masthead block, hoisting me up the mast in a breeches buoy in driving rain. We still couldn't convince our expensive weather fax to work, a program that was supposed to print current weather patterns miles ahead. After two days of frustration, we gave up. No weather fax for us.

We skipped the annual cruiser's Christmas/New Year's Eve party and went to bed early because Joe on *Endeavor* was getting married the next day, on New Year's Eve. The weather was glorious at the old *ranchero*, and presto, Joe became foreman of a cattle operation, five houses, five families, and an intricate irrigation system. We gorged ourselves on the excellent buffet and liberally sampled the open bar, staggering back to *Grendel* at midnight.

9

January 1994

At 4 a.m. an explosion rocked the dock and woke us up. We jumped on deck and wobbled to the adjoining dock to witness every sailor's number one nightmare. A raging fire. *Windsong* had blown up, followed by a second explosion and an out-of-control fire. I joined five other cruisers sharing two garden hoses, trying to put out the fire. But fiberglass creates a blistering inferno, too hot to even approach.

When Jimmy, *Windsong*'s owner, appeared, the mast fell. Jimmy climbed on board and refused to leave the burning deck, playing the staunch captain going down with his ship. A blonde lady ran up, yelling the fire was all her fault, and launched into what in other circumstances would have been an entertaining screaming match with Jimmy. I didn't know her name but knew she lived on a boat next to Abe's at a marina a few miles south of town. She was shacking up with someone other than Jimmy, who screamed at her to get the hell away from *Windsong*. It took dozens of cruisers to coax Jimmy off the burning hulk. He finally dove into the water when *Windsong* began drifting into a powerboat in the next berth.

Cruisers fended off the burning hulk until the La Paz fire department belatedly arrived. But the fire truck couldn't get close to the fire because the marina had installed a new combination lock, and no one knew the code. When we got the gate open, the fire department had forgotten to bring water, so we watched *Windsong* burn to the waterline. The carcass slid into the bay with an anticlimactic hiss, bringing an abrupt end with plumes of acrid smoke. Happy New Year. It was rumored Jimmy's bank had tried to repo *Windsong* twice, and the fire was arranged to collect on insurance.

We ordered mail, waiting to leave La Paz until delivered by our Florida mail-forwarding service. After a week, we decided it must have gotten lost. We still couldn't get the weather fax to work and Mary was becoming increasingly frustrated with random failures of equipment and my less than well-laid plans. Little was open on New Year's Day, so we wandered around town, visiting random bars at fancy hotels, imbibing huge margaritas at La Perla. Mary had two drinks, making her several sheets to the wind, and we fell into bed at 9:30 p.m., beyond ready to get out of La Paz.

When I gave up trying to fix the electric foot pump, Mary suggested it'd only lost its prime. We removed it, filled it with water, and reinstalled it, and it worked great. Mary had a far better mechanical sense than I did, illustrating my desperate need for help on the boat!

We tried the weather fax program on a friend's computer, using his modem, and then my modem, and it worked fine. We took it back to *Grendel* and it wouldn't work at all. Late on January 6, the mail arrived, and two days later we were ready to sail. We celebrated leaving La Paz with friends with an El Cortijo dinner. Mazatlán, here we come after I'd spent six and a half months in La Paz.

We left at high tide on January 8, *Grendel*'s reefed mainsail close-hauled, making about one knot. Though we'd vowed to never run the engine when we had enough wind to sail, we fired it up anyway. The RPMs maxed out at 1800, which was pitiful, though we somehow reached a normal five-knot cruising speed. As we sailed into Caleta Lobos to anchor for the night, I dropped the heavy anchor in fifty-five feet of water, and the engine died.

Mary handled the anchor while I maneuvered the boat the next morning, grunting and groaning, cursing like the sailor she'd smoothly become. After endless grinding, the engine started and then died, and it felt permanent. We had to return to La Paz to consult Pablo and figure out what the hell had gone wrong this time.

After restarting the engine, the RPMs were so low that it took three hours to motor back to La Paz. Pablo showed up the next day and suggested we clean the carburetor and change the fuel filter. We did, and the engine ran fine. Total cost: $16.67, plus slip fees and two more days lost.

The wind piped up that night, and Mary lost her enthusiasm for leaving the next morning. Still, we got up at 6 a.m. and started the engine. I ran to say goodbye to the neighbors, and they were horrified we were leaving in such high winds, so we didn't. Mary was again disappointed.

While waiting for the wind to abate, Mary ran into an old boyfriend named Bill O'Connor. He'd flown down to crew on *Hot Toddy*, a neighboring boat. We spent several hours with Bill and other cruisers, poring over *Grendel*'s charts, marking the best anchorages between Mazatlán and Manzanillo. Mary and Bill originally met in Phoenix when he remarked on her exceedingly attractive legs.

The wind moderated to thirty knots at 2:30 p.m., gusting to forty, and Mary wanted to leave. Our cruising buddies said they wouldn't sail in that much wind, so we stayed another night. The next day was the same, lots of gusty wind with breakers onshore. We got around to leaving La Paz on the 15th, a week after our first try, and a month after we'd intended. Ah, the idyllic sailing life.

With little wind, we motored four hours to our first anchorage. Morning broke without a drop of wind. To avoid motoring, we waited for the wind to pipe up, sitting on anchor as *Grendel* rolled through eighty to ninety degrees of sheer vertigo. A twenty-five-knot breeze blew up at noon, sculpting giant rollers the Tillermaster couldn't handle, blowing six fuses during five hours while trying to keep *Grendel* on course. Since we were running out of fuses, we had to hand-steer, which was exhausting. The sky was gray, overcast, and ultra-depressing with nothing going right, which is what sailing often seems to boil down to.

We dropped the sails and anchored, but couldn't sleep because the boat was rolling through ninety degrees, continuing for eleven hours. The motion was so extreme I thought the mast would collapse, and the bikes and emergency life raft would fly off the deck. The pounding below decks felt like out-of-control thunder, and when magnified by the hull, sounded like endless rammings by a squadron of whales.

We fell out of bed the next morning and found the cabin filled with everything we'd so carefully stowed: books, magazines, clothes, manuals, and office supplies. The severe rolling had emptied every compartment, creating a tangle of clothing and provisions that blocked access to everything from the radar to the refrigerator and watermaker. We sat dazed, mentally and physically unable to clean up the mess, in shock at the surrounding disaster, ready to pack it in and buy an RV instead.

We were exhausted and bruised, made worse because when refueling the outboard motor I again spilled fuel in the cockpit. I sent Mary back to bed and took the tiller, tearing up at the futility of actually sailing around the world. My first command decision was to skip two days on our intended course, 113 nautical miles to Isla Isabella. Instead, we'd sail directly across the Sea of Cortez to Mazatlán, sixty-nine miles away. I spent the next eight hours hand-steering, unwashed, existing on power bars, making Mary stay below and rest, only able to trim the sails and keep *Grendel* on an approximate course.

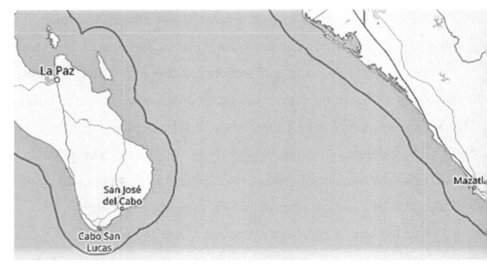

La Paz to Mazatlán

The seas calmed, and we had a halfway decent night's sleep. The next morning, we motored in placid sunlight, both of us in shock, slumped in the cockpit. We ignored the clogged cabin, too tired to do more than take turns on the tiller and trim the sails, hoping to reach Mazatlán in a few hours, back to civilization and away from the endless ocean. The timing meant approaching an unknown port at night, but the GPS and radar took us right to the harbor's mouth, where I turned behind the wrong breakwater. This mistake cost two long, frigid hours, and we anchored at 9:30 p.m. instead of 7:30 as planned. Mary was wet and cold, crying in frustration and exhaustion but it was sheer joy to anchor in a protected harbor with no roll or swell, able to enjoy nicely warmed sun showers on deck. We lathered up, washed off in lovely hot water, and fell into bed.

Mazatlán

The first boat we saw the next morning was *Bustamante* with Kay and Tom on board, also originally from Phoenix. We'd met them in La Paz and knew they'd planned to leave for Mazatlán one day after we did. Tom was a journeyman carpenter, highly skilled, and had met Kay in high school. They'd been inseparable ever since. We rowed into shore for a radio-arranged meeting, and with the first pull on the oar, the oarlock broke. Expletive deleted. Once ashore, we checked in with the port captain and immigration as required at every Mexican port.

I called the Tillermaster company after Mary swore we had to get it fixed to avoid hand steering, or she was *outa there*. I wholeheartedly agreed. Without a working autopilot, sailing wasn't worth the effort. The Tillermaster company offered to expedite mail fuses, so I ordered a hundred slow-blow one-and- a-half-amp fuses, super-fast delivery to Mazatlán prepaid. Because Tillermaster's so-called slow-blow fuses had never been slow to blow, I suggested they pop them up to two amps and take a walk on the wild side.

We spent a day with Kay and Tom walking around Mazatlán, each of us with a shopping list. Kay and Tom's shopping list included kitschy salt and pepper shakers collected by their son while our lists were for a new oarlock and slow-blow one-and-a-half-amp fuses. We confirmed that slow-blow one-and-a-half-amp fuses do not exist in Mexico, Mexican salt and pepper shakers are insufficiently kitschy, and oarlocks are always sold on the other side of town.

Our little group ran into George on *Guilty*, a Scottish chap about age sixty-five, and found that his bad luck eclipsed ours. George had lost his steering while sailing down from San Diego and had been way overcharged for repairs at the expensive Cabo marina. Someone had stolen his dinghy in Cabo, his sails had been ripped in a storm, and he'd given up. George was heading back to San Diego tomorrow. It cheered us up enormously to find someone worse off than we were.

Finally, some fun. Off with Kay and Tom to Senor Frog's, which Mary and I had visited in Mazatlán years before. We arrived at 6 p.m. and found the dining room full. No one was in the bar except four *gringos*, but Senor Frog's gradually filled up and got rowdy when an old guy about eighty and his sixtyish girlfriend, began dancing their asses off. They did jumping jacks, twists, and push-ups, enthralling everyone.

111

Someone passed a blonde lady hand-to-hand down our table. Why was a mystery but it likely had something to do with drinking way too much. We crashed before 10:30.

I got the oarlock repaired, again for five dollars, and we spent two days sewing mosquito netting to fit over the hatches and companionway, trying to keep the pesky little buggers out of the cabin.

After the trauma at sea, we recuperated by spending a week exploring the Mazatlán area by bus, going with Kay and Tom to Copola, a quaint Mexican hilltop village and four hundred-year-old mining town with narrow cobblestone streets. A lone pig sauntered down the main street, and a kid on a donkey posed for pictures. The small square contained an ancient church, which fascinated religious Kay. We had banana cream and coconut pie with beer at Daniel's, a restaurant overlooking a ravine filled with wild mango trees and parrots, owned by an ex-pat named Daniel.

Back in Mazatlan, we rowed to shore for dinner and a breaker swamped the dinghy, a reoccurring drenching that always pissed Mary off. Every single time, and rightly so. A radio message from Club Nautica partially relieved this disaster because our elusive one-and-a-half-amp slow-blow fuses had arrived for the Tillermaster, which we'd voted the most important component on the boat. Customs duties raised the cost by a third, but big-spenders us ordered twenty more fuses.

Grendel's batteries refused to hold a proper charge, and it took us two days to figure out why. The solar panels weren't generating enough electricity to power both the watermaker and the refrigerator. We needed more panels, which weren't available in Mexico. We could charge the batteries only by running the engine every day or fly to San Diego and buy more solar panels. We spent hours discussing whether to give up cruising, find more solar panels, run the engine daily, or find a wind generator. Mary also coveted a backup Tillermaster, and a better dinghy, tired of our dinghy perpetually swamping, which was mostly my fault.

We rowed into shore to clear immigration and customs, ready to leave Mazatlán, when the oarlock broke again. I'd lost count of how many times this had happened. Another re-weld job, after which we re-anchored to make water in a cleaner corner of the harbor. We rafted up with four other boats and rowed into shore to watch the Super Bowl at a beach palapa. When the game began, we left to walk around town and decided to sail to Isabella Island with Kay and Tom, excited to leave Mazatlán. When we dinghied back to the boat, the outboard wouldn't shut off, but Kay and Tom rode to our rescue. My supreme talent was whatever is the opposite of seamanship.

When we left for Isabella, the Tillermaster went off course and I thought we'd blown a fuse. We hadn't, but Mary repeated her suggestion that we sell the boat and buy an RV instead. RVs are much easier to navigate than dealing with the daily hazard of lee shores, dragging anchors, no wind or too much wind, and an endless list of other perils and continuous repairs. I'd kick in $20,000 and Mary would borrow the same amount from her dad. We were sure we'd find a great RV but speculated, based on our natural competency, that we might drive the RV off a cliff. We'd stick with cruising until we made it through the Panama Canal into the Caribbean. Pipe dreams were us.

Isabella Island was a bust. We arrived at dawn, motored around the island to the east side where *Slipaway*, who we'd met while watching the Super Bowl, was anchored, buffeted by unending surf and huge rolling waves. Crashing waves inundated the west side too, so we tried the south cove, but none of Isabella's anchorages were protected from wild surf. We were exhausted and too tired to continue sailing, so we anchored for a few hours and tried to nap. But it was like trying to sleep inside a washing machine, so we gave up at 11 a.m. and left for San Blas, knowing we'd arrive after dark. It was a gorgeous day away from land, but the rolling seas drove us and the Tillermaster nuts. Kay and Tom tolerated the surf longer than we were able, following in *Bastante* two hours later.

Mazatlán to Puerto Vallarta

10

February 1994

We dropped anchor in Matanchen Bay at 9:30 p.m., just south of San Blas, helped in by a strobe light on *Amalfia*. After a hot shower, Campbell's chicken noodle soup, and a can of fruit cocktail, we passed out. The next morning, we found that *Bastante* had arrived at 10:30 p.m., also helped onto anchor by *Amalfia's* strobe light.

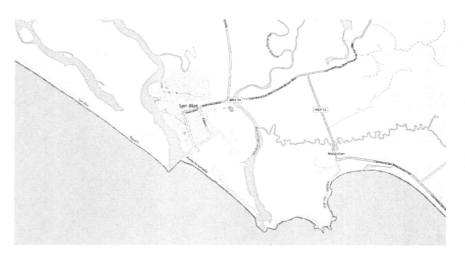

San Blas and Matanchen Bay

The next morning we tried to check into Immigration and the Port Authority in San Blas, along with *Bastante,* but all government offices were closed. We settled for lunch at McDonald's: grilled chicken, enchiladas, chips, beans, and guacamole with salsa. Five dollars for four people. A San Blas religious festival and parade began right after lunch with participants dressed as crocodiles and crocodile disciplinarians, men with whips herding fake crocodiles. A local explained this was a talisman to keep the thousands of alligators where they belonged, in the swamps surrounding San Blas, instead of wandering around town.

Fake alligators were followed by cloggers clomping and young girls wearing gold tinfoil crowns and capes stenciled with the Virgin Mary. The next float featured a priest holding a scroll with a young girl kneeling in front of him. We didn't ask why, though it looked mighty suspicious. Catholic Kay studiously ignored our comments. The parade's next three hours featured hundreds of townspeople carrying candles.

A bishop presided over the next day's parade, which was made up of bow and arrow clackers, a torch lighting ceremony, and fireworks. The bishop blessed each boat in the harbor, accompanied by an ancient wooden statue of St. Blaze, the patron saint of San Blas. We filled *Grendel*'s water tanks, distracted by the bishop until the tanks overflowed and soaked a dozen books in the cabin below. Sopping-wet books included the primary source reference for the new book I was writing and the only copy of my first published book.

For a panoramic view of the surrounding mangrove swamps, we climbed to a fort overlooking San Blas, and then visited the local cemetery, which was decorated with ornate tombs, tiny glasshouses, and statuary. There we met Jose, the local gravedigger, who showed us two American graves, one of which he proclaimed a "*Juden*." He gave us a tour of his living quarters in the cemetery, a ragged hammock on the verge of collapse. For his daily meal, Jose grilled a hot dog on rusty rebar, next to his only possessions--a pan of grease, and a half-full Coca-Cola. Eight kids swam in the muddy estuary next to the cemetery, grubbing for oysters to sell at local restaurants, making the oysters I'd eaten the day before less than appetizing.

Mexican prices continued to amaze. A sumptuous dinner of ceviche, fish and shrimp tacos and quarts of beer cost thirteen dollars for four people. Eleven cruisers signed up for an all-day five-dollar trip to local waterfalls and an all-day tour of the mangrove swamps and crocodile farm for seven dollars. Locals sold delicious loaves of bread: banana was the most popular, rivaled by pineapple, carrot, and coconut--all delicious.

The jungle tour glided through narrow mangrove tunnels, scraping the panga on both sides. As we meandered through twists and turns as mysterious as Tom Sawyer's cave, the guide pointed out every species of jungle bird. We spotted white egrets, fat turtles sunning on dappled tree trunks, and hovering black egrets. Dull brutish alligators lurked on the banks, creatures from the underworld similar to the twenty-pound catfish swimming silently below us. We slid by an enormous tree chock-full of white buzzards, uglier than the black red-headed kind, before arriving at an enormous spring that was the source of the San Blas water supply, a gigantic pool of freshwater flanked by tall white lilies next to the crocodile farm. Our guide tied up at a fancy restaurant where we had lunch, flanked by the water pumping station. The day was capped off for me when we were seated next to a family whose teenage son wore a Phoenix Suns jersey.

Cruisers organized a potluck of beer and volleyball on the beach, attended by thirty folks from ten boats. Ten cruisers from *Grendel, Quo Vadis, Bastante,* and *Yolo* went on the waterfall trip the next morning. Pepe, the proprietor of El Albatross Restaurante on the beach, was our guide to the waterfall. We piled into the back of his ramshackle pickup. It took an hour to pass sixteen RVs in a caravan winding into the tropical hills above San Blas. The last five miles were on a rough dirt road to El Caro, a minuscule village with a tiny church, a *mercado*, and a school overrun by a multitude of pigs, horses, chickens, and turkeys with no *gringos* or tourist shops to be seen.

During the first twenty minutes of our hike to the waterfall, Pepe became hopelessly lost, but half an hour later we stumbled onto a 250-foot-wide pool fed by an eighty-foot waterfall. After a box lunch, we trekked to a lookout with a vista over the valley, which included two more waterfalls with milky-green water flowing over copper-colored rocks, surrounded by banana, papaya, and bamboo trees. Back at Pepe's restaurant, we feasted on ceviche shrimp tacos and beer while inundated with no-see-ums, bitey little bastards, against which there is no defense.

The next morning, we motored *Grendel* twenty miles to Chacala, accompanied the first hour by a school of three-foot mackerel, sailing in brilliant sunshine on calm and clear seas, almost making up for previous sailing nightmares. We anchored off a pristine beach with four fellow travelers including *Bastante* and *Quo Vadis,* surrounded by jungle, and *Quo Vadis* landed an enormous fish. The beach was lined with ten dinky restaurants with a pier for landing dinghies. After dinner, six-foot swells rocked and rolled us all night, making us miserable and unable to sleep.

We sat on our respective boat decks in the middle of a pod of whales that swam around the lagoon, breaching, twisting, and spouting, enjoying the washing machine effect that drove us nuts.

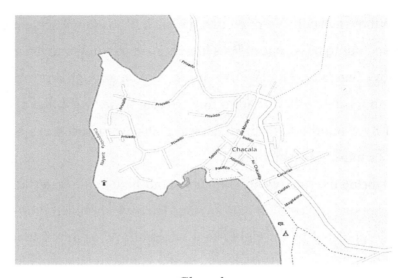

Chacala

We were tired and grumpy the next morning so *Grendel* and *Bastante* upped anchor and moved to the lee of an island off Punta Rosa, next to four Mexican shrimp boats on a small bay that was calm and less grump-inducing. Our other two compatriots continued south along the Mexican mainland, heading for La Cruz just past the entrance to Bahia de Banderas and Puerto Vallarta, which was miles away at the protected end of the bay. Sailing charts in this part of Mexico were off by two miles in random directions, making for tenuous navigation.

We still hadn't decided when we would quit cruising, but we thought we'd sail as far as Costa Rica and through the Canal to the

Caribbean by April, agreeing to invest no more money in *Grendel*. Both decisions were make-believe.

Though jammed with two dozen boats, La Cruz was a gorgeous location. We anchored close to shore in nine feet of water, setting stern and aft anchors near a sunken shrimper. Restaurant Don Felipe offered inexpensive hamburgers and margaritas at tables with white tablecloths and HBO on a giant TV under a spacious palapa with views of the Bay of Banderas. In the misty distance we could see Bucerias, Nuevo Vallarta, and Puerto Vallarta.

La Cruz and Bucerias

The cruisers organized a swap meet at Nuevo Vallarta, eight miles by road, where we salivated over a hundred-amp alternator. Our alternator had stopped working, but we passed on the luscious hundred-amper because we'd vowed to put no more money into the boat. Cruisers we hadn't seen since La Paz stopped by to say hi: *Just Us, Erio,*

Chardonnay, and *Wunderbar II*. That afternoon, a fifty-foot French boat named *Vento,* worth well over a half-million dollars, broke loose of its anchor and began drifting until rescued by fellow cruisers.

We sailed into Nuevo Vallarta's marina to rent a slip so we could explore the Mexican interior, ending up next to *Puffin* and *Sundown*, cruisers we knew. The biggest drawback to cruising, excluding unending boat repairs, weather disasters, and trauma for the mechanically and electrically challenged, is exploring the interior of a country. This required leaving *Grendel* in a secure marina, where we also had to catch up on chores, charge the house batteries, find a new alternator or get ours fixed, repair the erratic now demoted to Demi-God Tillermaster, wash the boat inside and out, do laundry, order eyeglasses, clean the bottom, attend Carnival, provision, and check-in with Customs and Immigration. Then we could head to Guadalajara.

Nuevo Vallarta to Puerto Vallarta

Expensive condos, restaurants, and upscale shops surrounded the Nuevo Vallarta marina, which contained over three hundred boats, almost all far more expensive than *Grendel*. The shower and bathroom facilities were grossly inadequate for the number of boats, and the closest bus to town was two miles away. After riding it once, crammed with raucous mariachi buskers, we unpacked the bikes.

Our mail arrived and the bank statement imposed overdraft charges, though it failed to list any overdrafts. The bank had accidentally processed a $6,000 check to the I.R.S. twice. In these pre-Skype days, we had to write the bank, along with postcards to cruiser friends in La Paz, while working on the boat for three busy days. Tom on *Bastante* built an extension to our spacious forward berth, making it a fabulous playpen. At 7 a.m. the next morning we headed to Guadalajara with Kay and Tom.

We were late for the bus we'd selected, but luxury buses left for Guadalajara every hour. The route wound through endless agave fields and the town of Tequila, where vendors crowded the bus selling commemorative flasks and potato chips. We stayed in downtown Guadalajara at Hotel Hamilton for seventy-five pesos, aka eighteen dollars, buying two double beds in a room perfect for cheap cruisers. We spotted a few cockroaches, but the shower had hot water that drained nicely, and the toilet had a seat. Not bad, but we changed hotels anyway, hoping for fewer roaches.

Guadalajara was a delightful city with historical monuments, potato chip vendors, and mammoth plazas with sprawling cathedrals. Folks crowded sidewalks, watching television through store windows crammed with Catholic paraphernalia. We found a shopping center as big as the Mall of America that included a reflecting pool, a white-tie wedding spilling over the sidewalk, dozens of yogurt stalls and shoe stores, and the largest *mercado* in Mexico. We switched hotels to the Posada San Pablo, where breakfast cost $12.50 for two, the most cheapskates Mary and I had ever spent. Coffee was three dollars plus seventy-five cents for cream, refills extra. We fled the restaurant but loved the hotel with its nine two-story rooms built around a courtyard filled with exotic birds and tropical plants, only twenty-five dollars for four. We ate breakfast at Denny's.

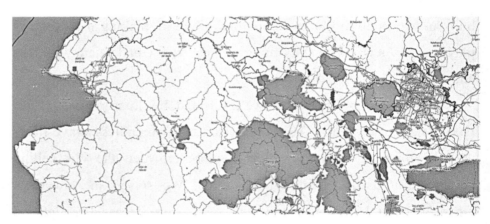

Puerto Vallarta to Guadalajara, Tlaquepaque and Chapala

The close-by town of Tlaquepaque was a *don't miss*, built around a sprawling plaza. Chic shops sold ceramics, metal works, leather, and exotic wood sculptures ranging from gorgeous to grotesque. The many bars and restaurants offered garden seating, where we stuffed our faces with a whole roast chicken, coleslaw, tortillas, and chiles for less than five dollars for four.

Next was Chapala on Lake Chapala, a *gringo*-retirement haven with luxury bus service from Guadalajara. The bus was served by an attractive stewardess and movies in English, thirteen dollars for the eighty-mile round trip. A haircut at the Chapala bus station cost three dollars, so I stepped right up. Afterward, we enjoyed lunch with butterflied grilled chicken and homemade ice cream, two scoops for a dollar. We strolled along the algae and ivy-choked lake that stretched to the hazy horizon and bought silly hats from sidewalk vendors. Mine sported a foot-long bill, and Mary's was adorned with a gaudy Tweety bird, pulling stares of awe from locals and laughter from gringo ex-pats. Junk food vendors sold fried sardines coated with chiles, gauzy women's clothing, ultra-cheap jewelry, and Peruvian tapas.

Tom flashed his Arizona Yacht Club (est.1958) membership card, and the Chapala Yacht Club admitted our party of four. The club boasted a soccer field, heated pools, and outside tables with umbrellas along a seawall. We quaffed beers among Mexican men wearing Italian suits and women bedecked with either diamonds or a ton of zircons. The luxury bus back to Guadalajara featured the movie *What About Bob?*. After multiple beers at the club, we found the movie uncommonly hilarious. In our brief absence, the air pollution in Guadalajara had increased to horrific. Departing planes disappeared into yellowy muck immediately after take-off. We avoided further eye irritation and sneezing by boarding the next luxury bus back to Puerto Vallarta.

The Nuevo Vallarta marina had run out of fuel, but the manager assured us there was a definite possibility fuel might be delivered tomorrow, a common hedge in Mexico. We'd planned to sail the next morning, but only with full fuel tanks and the lack of fuel delayed our departure for three days. We whiled away the time with a weather fax class (we were still unable to get ours to work) and trips to a sprawling fruit and veg market while spiffing up the boat.

Mary was eager to leave and was unable to relax so I tried hitchhiking five miles from the Nuevo Vallarta marina to the Pemex in Bucerias to fill our gas cans. I stood at the edge of the road yelling, "quince," meaning "fifteen," easily getting a ride to and from the gas station. I was happy to return with full gas cans, only to tussle with the driver over whether I'd offered him *quince*/fifteen in pesos or dollars. Pesos, of course, which would have been five dollars. We settled on twenty pesos at the exact moment when the long-awaited gasoline truck arrived to fill the marina's fuel tanks.

We left Nuevo and sailed into the Puerto Vallarta (PV) estuary, where the damn alternator stopped charging, again. I removed the alternator to schlep it into town for repairs, and when we arrived back on board, Mary had forgotten the key to unlock the boat. So, we borrowed a screwdriver to dismantle the lock. The day's only bright spot was a walking tour of old town PV with Kay and Tom where boats paraded around the inner harbor, featuring everything from ferries, pangas, and dinghies to fishing boats, dive boats, and fancy yachts.

An after-parade cruiser party at Dos Felipe's in Santa Cruz offered a chili cookoff with kegs of frosty beer, and Tom offhandedly mentioned tomorrow was March 1. We were stunned, having lost all track of time. The only thing on our calendar was the month of June when we'd vowed to decide whether to continue to Costa Rica or turn around and head back up to San Diego, giving up on this crazy cruising idea. The highlight was watching the Suns/Knicks game where Barkley got kicked out for fighting with the Knicks' Anthony Mason, but the Suns won so life was good.

11

March 1994

The next morning, we took a bus to downtown PV to check in with immigration. The head honcho arrogantly told us we had to first check in with Customs in an office five miles north of the city. We spent all morning shuttling back and forth on PV buses with Mary was more annoyed than I was. I delivered the repaired alternator back in the dinghy, but stepped off-center and swamped it. GI got wet from the waist down, and worse, I'd done no favors for the alternator, but I thanked Poseidon that Mary wasn't in the dinghy.

That evening with Kay and Tom, they'd rented *What About Bob?* to watch a second time in commemoration of our giddy trip to Chapala. We unanimously realized while watching the movie sober that it was really stupid.

Since we had ample time to sightsee, we caught a packed bus to Mismaloya Beach where *Night of the Iguana* was filmed. Sunbathers packed the beach, harassed by dozens of vendors, which we escaped by investing in dollar beers and hiking to an abandoned hilltop castle. Back on shore, a spastic *gringo* tried surfing with a cast on his arm and was dumped on a wave. He washed up on the beach with a severe case of sand up his butt. He scooped seawater up his shorts, trying to wash the sand out with one hand while his bikinied girlfriend snapped candid photos. We and other bystanders gave him a standing ovation.

Back at the marina, Kay and Tom received their mail and were ready to leave PV to sail south. This spurred Mary and me to list what we'd need to continue cruising: a stable dinghy, a new Tillermaster or wind vane pilot, and GPS. These would cost at least $8,300. Then add the time and effort it'd take to find a properly sized dinghy and wind vane and get the items to Mexico We decided it was too much work to sail around the world, or even around Mexico. To avoid the unending hassles of lee shores, spotty electronics, an incompetent captain, exorbitant customs duties, and unending red tape, we decided to buy an RV and see the world that way instead.

When Mary called her son and parents to tell them we were returning to sell the boat, her father sprung a surprise. He invited her to join a two-week family expedition in May to Greece with her three sisters and assorted aunts, all expenses paid by her dad and uncles. To picture her Greek family, think of *My Big Fat Greek Wedding*. Mary's dad was the Greece-uber-alles banty rooster mirror image of the father in the movie. Naturally, Mary would love to go to Greece for two weeks, and I wouldn't mind staying with the boat, wherever it'd be at the time. Afterward, we'd sail to San Diego and sell *Grendel* for whatever price we could get, investing the proceeds in an RV somewhere in the world.

I'd been RVing for twenty-five years, buying the first one in 1969 immediately after graduation from law school from the Volkswagen Campervan factory in Wiedenbruck, Germany. My first wife and I drove it around Europe for three months, including through occupied East

Germany, before shipping it back to Phoenix. I had a lot more experience with RVs than with sailboats.

When we walked over to swim in the pool, the PV marina and yacht club was being decorated for a bash, but we had to flee from staring workmen and the sensation caused by Mary in her new one-piece swimsuit. We escaped to La Cruz by bus to attend a cruisers' dart tournament at Don Felipe's, where we'd agreed to meet Kay and Tom. A hundred cruisers attended the party, including a dozen we knew, the majority by their boat names. We saw *Sweet Lorraine*, who we'd met in Mazatlán, and attended Carnival together.

It seemed an eternity ago that we'd met Patty and Derek on *Just Us* and Terry on *Eye of Infinity*, the *professional idiot* who I'd first met in June when slinking into La Paz. *Song of Joy* from Camp Verde, Arizona, had given us a ride from PV to NV two weeks before, and we'd met *Yaqui* in San Blas. He'd signed up to crew on *Verité*, the day after it'd dragged anchor in Mazatlán. Favorites included Tom and Nancy on *M'Lady*, Terry and his sister Donna on *Puffin*, Joe on *Dijana*, and Gil on *Dionysius*, who'd permanently left his former partner in PV. The cruising world was small and close-knit, always ready to help another cruiser with a problem, which was the only reason I'd survived this long.

We rolled out of our bunk at 3 a.m., ready to sail away at 5 a.m. Kay and Tom planned to depart two hours later. They'd kindly put off leaving until our mail arrived because they knew we always needed help to escape my next inevitable blunder. It took six hours to reach the end of the thirty-mile-long bay and dip our toes into the Pacific Ocean, where three-foot-high rollers swept around Cape Corrientes. With little wind to

130

stabilize her, *Grendel* rolled through ninety degrees ad nauseum, and Mary was seasick for the first time I could remember.

When *Brenda Jane* and *Kathy Lee* rounded the point ahead of us, *Bastante* was five miles behind. We celebrated passing *Brenda Jane*, who was sailing a leisurely wing and wing, anchoring next to *Kathy Lee*. The surf was rolling too much to sleep, pitching and surging *Grendel* with giant waves that exploded on the beach, over a half-exposed wreck behind us, and in geysers over the rocky point. An attractive restaurant and bar beckoned onshore, surrounded by cute, tiny houses, but we couldn't take the dinghy through the surf without swamping it.

Three kids in a panga motored out, one yelling. "Twenty pens and paper, mister, for school." We had no pencils or writing paper, but we gave them candy, an exception for us, which the kids overly appreciated. After decades of travel, we'd learned to never give candy to kids because those in poorer countries received little or no dental care, so the candy would cause rotten teeth and poor health. After a night with no sleep, we sailed away at 6 a.m., but the alternator was on the fritz again. So, we turned around, taking 8 hours to re-anchor at four p.m. in La Cruz. This naturally disgusted Mary, and I was irritated that she was disgusted.

After endless diagnoses and failed repairs, we bought a seventy-amp alternator. According to the chap who sold it to us, the alternator had been salvaged from a 1979 Cadillac in South Philly. Unfortunately, it wouldn't fit on the engine, so we spent ten dollars to fabricate a mount to make it work. Poor Barry off *Sunrise* was frustrated for days, trying to jury-rig the alternator to fit inside the engine compartment while juggling a half-dozen other projects, and seldom able to show up when promised. Kay and Tom contacted us via the cruiser's net, letting us know they were headed to Melaque, twenty-four hours of non-stop sailing away.

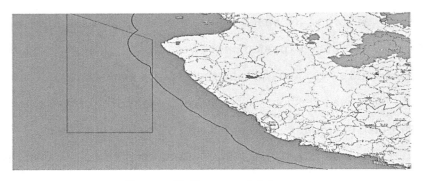

Puerto Vallarta to Melaque

At 6 a.m. the next day, we left for Melaque on the high tide. Five hours later, as we approached Cape Corrientes and the open ocean, we smelled the stink of burning rubber. My heart dropped when I saw the batteries weren't charging and I ran below to the engine room to find a shredded alternator belt. This meant turning around for repairs--again. I dowsed the jib and tried to raise the staysail, but it was stuck at the masthead. I tried to climb the mast but couldn't climb more than halfway up, to the spreaders, because each passing wave was swinging the fifty-foot mast through thirty feet of arc, threatening to throw me into the surf.

We crept back to Nuevo Vallarta, and had to wait for three hours until high tide made the channel deep enough so we could enter the harbor. After forty-five minutes, I became impatient and sailed in. I was in a funk and Mary was shaking, afraid we'd go aground, though trying her damnedest to be optimistic and supportive. Twelve strenuously wasted hours later, we were back to where we'd started early that morning.

When we came into the harbor, Barry heard us on the net and was waiting on the dock when we tied up. He examined the tattered fan belt and prescribed a shorter one, driving us downtown where we bought two. I had to climb the mast twice, first to free the halyard and the second time to WD-40 the mast-top pulley, an easy job in a calm marina without the mast whipping around like a fifty-foot crack-the-whip.

I sent a fax to Bud, a delivery captain in La Paz, asking whether he could help deliver *Grendel* from Cabo or La Paz to San Diego. We wanted to leave on April 5 or June 1, before or after Mary's family trip to Greece. Meanwhile, Barry had the alternator working in twenty minutes. We retired for beers with other cruisers, deciding to give Melaque a third try in the morning. We also ordered more Tillermaster fuses for delivery to the Las Hadas Resort Hotel and Marina in Manzanillo, commonly used by cruisers for mail forwarding. Fuses and items without printed matter could be delivered without inspection by Mexico City Customs.

Marina Vallarta called to report a fax from Bud, who confirmed he was available to help deliver *Grendel* to San Diego in April or June. Though we'd hoped to attend Race Week in the Sea of Cortez, Mary said April 5 would be best, getting it done and over with. Several years before, we'd chartered a boat and participated in La Paz Race Week, a cruisers' delight with countless absurd and risqué drinking games. Now we tussled with mixed feelings with three weeks to decide which date would be better. We loved exotic places and the many cruisers we'd met, but hated wasting so much time snagging and importing parts, and making constant repairs. In addition, Mary had no time or adequate place to jog or exercise, and I didn't either. Worse from my viewpoint, I had no time to write. Bud's price for helping deliver *Grendel* was $600 plus airfare back to La Paz, totaling about $900.

There was no wind on the way to Melaque so we motored for twenty-six hours nonstop, arriving beat with very little sleep after two-hour watches. When we arrived, in commemoration of St. Patrick's Day a priest was blessing boats in the harbor. The Irish were a major population in Mexico, having settled cities such as Ciudad Obregon, City of O'Brian south of Guaymas. Mexico always jumped on any excuse for a celebration.

We anchored three times in the howling wind before finding a suitable spot, during which the priest blessed *Grendel* twice. It seemed like we always had too little wind to sail and too much wind on anchor. Mary was miserable with the constant rolling, pitching, and tossing, having to constantly grab whatever handhold was available to avoid falling overboard. Kay and Tom stopped by to say hi, and we dinghied to shore for a St. Patrick's Day party at Philomena's bar on the beach, one of five bars at that end of town.

Fueled by dollar drinks, the party at Philomena's was out of control. A dozen guys mooned the restaurant from the beach and the local priest danced on a table. Folks wore giant oversized condoms on their heads and humongous dicks strapped to their waists, serenaded by bands you could hear half a mile away. You had to go outside to have a conversation. We left early to fax Bud, picking April 5 to take *Grendel* back to San Diego. Mary wanted to fly him down to Melaque, so we could instantly switch to RVing the world.

After twenty-six hours of motoring and six hours of partying, we staggered back to the boat and collapsed. Mary tried to row the dinghy back to shore to tell Kay and Tom we wouldn't return for the rest of the party, but it swamped in the surf. She returned wet and infuriated.

The next morning, we pulled up anchor to sail with *Bastante* and *Harmony* across the bay a few miles to Barra Navidad, but the engine wouldn't start, making Mary halfway hysterical. Until 4 p.m. I was unable to find Adam on *Brenda Jane* to look at the engine. He diagnosed the problem as a defective coil, which was easy to replace. A new coil only cost twelve dollars at a close-by auto-parts store, and the engine was running by 6 p.m. We motored over to Barra and anchored in a calm lagoon, a beautiful spot next to an unfinished resort hotel with a nicely trimmed golf course, and a ritzy housing development crisscrossed by canals. No rolling, calm as a pond, so we stayed for five days while waiting for the mail to arrive at the Las Hadas Hotel in Manzanillo.

The Barra dinghy landing was at the Sands Hotel, a fancy new place with immaculate gardens where staff mopped the tile floors ten times a day, or at least every time we traipsed through. The Sands had a giant pool with a terraced restaurant and charming palapa bar, offering happy hour from 2 p.m. to five every day with two margaritas for less than three dollars. Most of the happy hour attendees were cruisers, the cheapest tourists on the planet.

Kay's doctor had ordered lab tests, so we took a bus to Manzanillo the next day. While Kay was at the lab, we checked out the Las Hadas Hotel and Marina, where we hoped to anchor in a few days. If the mail was there when we arrived, we'd head back to La Paz, and that would be the last we'd see of Kay and Tom. We'd miss them as helpmates, close friends, and constant companions during the last three months.

The next morning, we bused to Tenacatita with two dozen cruisers, off to attend an awards ceremony sponsored by *Latitude 38* magazine out of San Francisco, the most popular cruising magazine in the U.S. The magazine had published my articles on cruising in Greece, Belize, and St. Vincent & The Grenadines, three of our seventeen sailing charters. The ceremony segued into a raucous cruiser's party with free-flowing booze, seemingly the key ingredient for every party everywhere.

The next day we bused to Las Hadas in Manzanillo, finding it reminiscent of Greek architecture, a spectacular hotel and marina, whitewashed and topped with blue-accented towers. The hotel's five-dollar margaritas and three-dollar beers shocked cheap cruisers us, but we downed several of each while getting to know other cruisers, such as Stan and Theresa on *Star Stuff* from Juneau. We found they knew Mary's first husband, an Alaska state cop who also lived in Juneau.

Back at the boat, we hosted Kay and Tom for what we thought would be our last supper together, a buffet on *Grendel*. They sailed the next morning for Las Hadas in Manzanillo as the first stop on their way to Costa Rico. Since we were headed the other direction this was the last we'd see thought we'd see of them for years. Our mail forwarding service in Florida promised mail delivery in three days by DHL to Las Hadas, but it'd been seven days and still no mail. DHL didn't deliver on weekends, so this being Friday and with a holiday on Monday, Tuesday would be the earliest we would get mail, almost two weeks after it'd been promised.

The only cheerful news was from Bud, our delivery captain, confirming he'd meet us in Cabo on April 5 to help deliver *Grendel* to San Diego. However, this changed the next day when Bud faxed to say he wouldn't be able to start the delivery until April 19 because his daughter was flying to La Paz for Race Week starting April 10. This meant that to begin her family trip to Greece, Mary would have to fly back to Phoenix from La Paz. We would need a minimum of three crew to cope with weeks of pounding into the teeth of permanent gale-force winds, which made Mary key to the delivery, delaying it until at least May.

Tom radioed the next day to let us know our mail had arrived at Las Hadas. Cost, sixty-six dollars. We jumped on the next bus to Manzanillo, surrounded by annual tropical fires. The locals burned the jungle every year to spur fresh growth during the upcoming hurricane season. Our bus drove through a fire raging across the highway, terrifying the passengers and prompting a shrug from the driver.

When we arrived, Tom and Kay told us the Las Hadas anchorage had been rolling badly the day before, so Tom helped us look for a better anchorage. Afterward, I bought another last meal for Kay and Tom. They stuck around for an hour, missing three buses going their way while we waited for a bus back to Barra, keeping us company one last time.

We started to sail north toward Mazatlán but had no wind for hours, stymied by high rollers and only able to make four knots against a one-knot current. Then the wind shifted from the north and we could only sail vaguely toward Mazatlán by tacking far off a northerly course, southwest toward Cabo. Wind always seemed to shift from the direction we wanted to go. At 1 p.m., the engine conked out and wouldn't restart, so I set a course to anchor in a nearby bay. Mary began crying, frustrated that we were sailing in the wrong direction to make an offing before heading north. Of course, I wasn't too happy either. However, I pointed out we were sailing an easy five knots, optimal speed for Grendel, even though way off course.

The wind rose over thirty knots, gusting to forty, and we lost momentum in the trough of the waves. When we'd top the swells, the sails would suddenly catch the wind, abruptly snapping and giving us whiplash. Then waves began crashing over the port side of the deck, and the bilge alarm rang. I closed the through-valve to the bilge but couldn't pump it dry. Water kept flooding the bilge, and Mary and I shared my familiar sinking feeling. I thought the water was coming from the outside drain into the cockpit, which I'd blocked months before, but it wasn't and the storm conditions made it impossible to find the source of the leak.

The only solution was to turn around and head back toward land and Barra. We scooted along depressed, still an hour from Barra when the sun set with a green flash. The Tillermaster was unable to hold a course across the high, rolling waves, and we were doubly exhausted by being unable to find the source of the leak that was slowly sinking the boat. We called for *Cathy Lee*, but she'd left. *September Song* answered instead, appearing in his dinghy to guide us through the narrow passage into Barra under reefed mainsail and shortened jib. We anchored at 8:30 p.m. in the same spot we'd vacated more than twelve hours before. The storm left us rung out and frustrated. I bagged the mainsail and jib, and we had popcorn for dinner, falling into bed at 10:30, shattered.

We dinghied in for breakfast and broke the choke switch on the outboard motor. Chris from *Yalani* inspected *Grendel's* electrical system while I searched for a replacement choke switch and faxed Bud, asking if he could help us deliver *Grendel* from Barra to La Paz before Race Week intervened. Chris inspected our new coil and said it was missing an external resistor. Like I knew it needed an external resistor, whatever that is, when I bought the dang thing! Chris replaced the points and adjusted the timing, so we bought dinner for *Yalani* and met up with *Scalawag* at Patty's, our favorite restaurant in Barra.

Chris gave us a ride to Melaque to buy the proper coil and replace the fuel we'd wasted yesterday, during which a slender, slightly drunk lesbian named Lucia from Guadalajara bought Mary a drink at the Sands bar. When I returned, Mary introduced me to Lucia, who was a character. We tried guessing Lucia's age, making her stand up and turn around, not too fast. What a cutie. Mary guessed forty, I guessed thirty-five, and Lucia kept swirling, saying she was twenty-eight. The gay and lesbian scene in Guadalajara was her favorite topic, a difficult situation in Mexico.

We left Lucia for a delightful dinner with *Yalani* and *Scalawag* and then were unable to start the outboard without a choke. We rowed back over the flat, calm lagoon under a full moon, an idyllic and stunning row of over a mile that took forty blissful minutes. The next morning, I corralled the outboard repair expert at the marina, but he had no replacement choke available. Only Mexico City might have one, but this was Easter week and everything was shut down. I found a plate to remount the broken choke on the outboard, hoping it'd last to La Paz. Tomorrow morning, we'd try sailing toward Mazatlán, again.

12

April 1994

The low tide was odd, twelve feet over average, giving us ample clearance through the narrow channel when we left the anchorage at 8:30 a.m. We waved goodbye to other cruisers and motored out to find flat seas, and were able to drop anchor in Matanchén Bay, accessible to San Blas, in only forty-eight hours. Because the normal intermediate stop at Chamela was often turbulent, we enjoyed the nicest two-day sail ever, straight through to San Blas. Naturally, we'd have our easiest passage as soon as we decided to quit sailing, the kind of passage everyone thinks sailing is all about. The engine, radar at night, and Tillermaster functioned perfectly as we lolled around, showering in the cockpit in brilliant sunshine, suffering the least amount of sailing stress ever.

We took three-hour watches the first night, refueled at sunup, and arrived at Cabo Corrientes before 7 a.m. The beautiful sunny weather complemented the calmest seas we'd ever sailed, and the half-moon helped spot shrimpers lurking at night. However, a shrimper cut me off at 2 a.m. as we sailed into San Blas to anchor in Matanchén Bay, a quarter of a mile from other boats.

Rising at dawn we were surrounded by five boats, including *Carioca III*, with Alan and Susan, who I knew from La Paz. We shared a taxi to the San Blas Pemex to fetch fuel and found Easter-week traffic was bumper to bumper, which shut Mexico down every year. Ramshackle buses were standing room only and the backs of trucks were crammed with fiesta-goers. We arrived back at our dinghies with full gas cans and dashed through the surf without getting swamped, for a change. Whew, we'd made it by noon. We fell into our bunks, planning to once again sail toward Mazatlán at dawn.

The next morning, we turned north for the twenty-four to thirty-hour slog to Mazatlán while *Carioca III* headed south toward Costa Rica. He'd broken his exhaust manifold with my pipe wrench the night before and would have to fabricate a manifold or have one shipped from the states. We were so relieved to soon be done with that kind of problem. With a stiff breeze, the sailing weather was perfect and we made almost five knots under double-reefed mainsail. I was too lazy to hoist the jib. Less than two miles offshore, we set a direct 320-degree course for Mazatlán, figuring to arrive between 1 and 2 p.m. the next day. We had very little swell, small chop with a few whitecaps. Idyllic. Giving up on sailing depressed Mary, along with beginning the long slog back to San Diego, which would take weeks. I tried to cheer her up by listing all the problems we'd be leaving behind.

The finicky Tillermaster only went schizoid three times in three days, a good conduct record. We kept our fingers crossed that it'd keep working well, along with the radar, alternator, and recalcitrant coil. When sailing, we'd found far more can go wrong than can go right. We had to pump the bilge every four hours on the starboard tack, adding to Mary's foul mood. Still, giving up was for the best because we wouldn't otherwise have time to do what we loved: Mary exercising, reading, and lifting weights, and me writing, all difficult to impossible in heavy seas while juggling unending repairs. Sailing was boring, sickening, terrifying, or frustrating, far less often exhilarating, and just plain fun.

Our worst fear was what would break or go wrong next, especially without the skills or knowledge to fix anything and everything. We slowed to two knots in the afternoon chop, shaving two hours off our ETA, which we reset to 4 p.m. The boat rolled and swooped, but the motion slowed at sunset, and we were up to four knots by midnight, keeping three-hour watches. At 7 a.m., we refueled and sailed into a fog bank. At 11 a.m., the fog receded to the mainland and we sighted the Mazatlán harbor rock, four hours from the inner harbor. We had to pump the bilge every four hours and, with the stuffing box leaking profusely, had to open a seacock for drainage. The sailing was so easy that we had little to do on watch, which let Mary finish four books during the thirty-hour trip, improving her mood enormously.

I couldn't wait to anchor and go ashore, but I first had to fix the stuffing box and the engine blower, which had just quit. Without the blower, refueling would be dangerous because gasoline fumes were heavier than air and would collect in the bilge, going boom at the slightest spark. I checked the blower and stuffing box but didn't know how to fix either, so we anchored and organized a shore excursion, putting on sail covers, stowing anchors, and making sure all was shipshape. We gathered our laundry but instead of going ashore, collapsed on our bunk, catching up on sleep.

The next morning, we rowed into shore and found daylight-saving time made it an hour earlier than our clocks. We loved being back for breakfast at the very classy Santa Fe restaurant with its immaculate tiles and antique wood fixtures, our favorite near the marina. The breakfast special included fruit plates, French toast, Eggs Mexicana with frijoles and salsa, and bottomless hot coffee. Eight dollars for two.

I found yesterday's *Mexico City News*, the latest available, and Mary worked the crossword puzzle while I read. We hiked up the hill for a splendid view over the city and old town, cutting through the ramshackle Belmar Hotel to pick up our laundry. Mazatlan gave us two relaxed days of reading and we provisioned with enough groceries to last a week, though the crossing to Cabo or La Paz should only take two or three days.

With my mechanical skills, I'd made the stuffing box leak much worse. We hadn't written a single letter back to friends in the States because we were unable to confess that we'd turned around and weren't going to Costa Rico with other cruisers. Giving up. Unable to hack it!

We talked to Dixie on *Independence*, the boat that dragged in San Blas. They were worried about the weather forecast, postponing departure for another day because of high winds and a sea of whitecaps. Though we'd planned to leave, we also decided to wait another day. When we rowed in for breakfast at Restaurante Santa Fe, the water had calmed so we ate a hasty breakfast and rushed back to the boat, leaving in excellent sea conditions before 10:30 a.m.

We were worried about sailing through the nasty weather corner southeast of Cabo, where I'd broken the boom in the terrible June storm.

The other problem was relying on sails only because we didn't have quite enough fuel to motor all the way to Cabo. Something always lurked around the corner to ambush Captain Dave. On the plus side, the Tillermaster was working fine.

We faxed Bud about a Cabo rendezvous but had no confirmation he'd received it. Mary called a friend from her old job, Marsha Levy, and found she was flying down to Cabo for a week with her boyfriend John. Marsha suggested we meet up. We anticipated a week with friends, writing letters, and getting *Grendel* ready for the long trip to San Diego--also, unfortunately, having to do our taxes. Sailing to Cabo would be the last time we'd have to make a long passage on our own. What a relief.

The sail to Cabo turned out to be a smooth crossing with little or no wind, and we dropped anchor at 9:30 a.m., forty-eight hours after leaving Mazatlán. Bill on *Sundown* called to say hi and Terry on *Puffin* stopped by half an hour later, telling us about the rotten crossing they had on a straight shot from Puerto Vallarta. As seasoned sailors, we smiled sadly.

The last dregs of Mexico's two weeks of Easter Week buffeted the Cabo anchorage with jet skis, water skiers, and other crazies tearing up the bay. We anchored in twenty-three feet of water, a hundred yards off the Pueblo Bonito Hotel, a fancy resort with exotic birds, macaws, screechy peacocks, and colorful parrots. These noisy birds saturated the jungle-like grounds, where Mary's friend Marsha and John were staying. They proudly showed us their room, and we walked the half-mile to downtown Cabo for happy hour margaritas. We discovered the Suns/Seattle game would be on in the early afternoon the next day, and

I was excited because I hadn't seen the Suns for two months. Happy days were here again.

After our first day back in Cabo, the tourists left the bay, so we suffered neither jet skis nor turbulence when dinghying back to *Grendel*. I worked on the refrigerator and watermaker for two hours, then Mary took over. She turned an engine through-hull valve and had both running in fifteen minutes. Dang, good thing she'd come on the boat, or I'd have packed it in sooner. The Suns game was a disappointment, even over drinks and lunch at Squid Roe. The Suns were overtaken in the third quarter and soundly beaten by Seattle. Still, for me, to even watch a losing game was a nice change.

The wind piped up along with the surf, soaking us and the dinghy on the way back to *Grendel*. The wind and weather were worse the next day, with rolling surf and high, exhausting waves. We printed letters for Marsha and John to mail back in the States, but by late afternoon, we were tired and cranky, crashing early.

The next morning, John made a desperate request. He had to have some decent beer, which meant a case of Bud Light. We made fun of John's lack of taste but flagged down a Corona Beer Truck and bought him a case of his yuck, favorite beer for twenty-three dollars. I helped John carry the beer back to the hotel, lightening his mood remarkably. John and Marsha repeatedly asked us to sleep on their fold-out couch, and we repeatedly declined. Though they'd gotten smashed every night, they hadn't been sleeping well, waking every night at 2 a.m. I blamed the peacocks and Marsha blamed six margaritas, after which I wouldn't have been able to walk or stand.

John and Marsha had a jam-packed day planned with jet skiing in the morning and a super deluxe bungee jumping package for John in the afternoon—and he expected us to witness his exploits. The bungee package included a T-shirt, video, photo, and jump for fifty-five dollars. So, I climbed the tower with John, watching him get suited up and prepped. The jumpmaster called me Dad, and I considered punching him out. John described the first ten feet as sheer terror and declined a second jump for a mere ten dollars, special for him today. Afterward, I had to coax John down the 139-foot ladder.

We invited John and Marsha to tour *Grendel* and take a look at our life. To make sure they didn't get wet in our easy-to-swamp dinghy, we arranged a water taxi. *Grendel* impressed them as much more substantial while seeing it close up, compared to how small she looked bobbing on the bay a hundred yards outside their hotel window. We adjourned for happy hour at the Cabo Melia Hotel, finding the Suns/Nuggets game unavailable, so we reluctantly settled for the Bulls and the Nets, which was a lousy game, salvaged only by excellent drink deals. We left early because we had to move *Grendel* into the marina for three days. The ninety-seven-dollar price was a fortune for us, but necessary to make final preparations before Bud arrived to help take the boat up to San Diego.

We settled *Grendel* into a vacant marina slip, only the fourth boat in a marina with a hundred-boat capacity. Marina slip prices were exorbitant, catering only to desperate cruisers. While we washed down the boat, the gas delivery lady picked up five gas cans and filled them for fifty dollars, the price of the fuel plus five dollars. We didn't even have to schlep full cans back to the boat. A chap in the next slip, who was leaving for the South Pacific the next day, gave us a ride in his super-stable dinghy.

We endured two more nights of happy-hour parties with John and Marsha, starting with giant margaritas at Saltillos and hot fudge sundaes at Baskin-Robbins. We blew the next night at the Giggling Marlin, with a spaghetti dinner onboard *Grendel* afterward. The next morning, we escorted John and Marsha to the airport for their flight home. Such a relief. Socializing tired us out. The homily that all company stinks after three days shrank to one or two for us. We wanted no more social pressure and far less drinking because we had lots of work to get Grendel ready for a long, hard delivery into the teeth of the wind, waves, and current. We stocked up at the exorbitantly priced *supermercado*, blowing 181 pesos, over sixty dollars. Then we hosted a farewell happy hour for cruiser friends, Terry, Donna, and Bill, who were sailing to La Paz the next morning.

A half-hour before the Suns/San Antonio game, Bud showed up. He'd dropped his daughter at the Cabo airport and had only gotten three hours of sleep but was still excited after La Paz Race Week. Still, he was aghast that we thought the sail to San Diego would only take seven or eight days. He'd taken dozens of deliveries to San Diego and said it'd take twice as long if we were lucky. Of course, he was right, and we weren't lucky.

We'd have to motor all the way and didn't have enough fuel for the 430 nautical miles to Turtle Bay, the closest fuel on the eight hundred miles to San Diego. He ordered us to find and fill at least two more ten-gallon cans and four more fives, which meant withdrawing money at an ATM to buy the cans and the fuel. This took three hours. By 3:30 p.m. Bud was dog-tired, but he jumped in his car and drove 120 miles to La Paz to drop off his car and take a bus back to Cabo the next morning, leaving us with a list of chores.

Bud got back to Cabo at noon the next day, and we sailed out of the marina at 2:30 p.m., off for San Diego and the end of our sailing dream. By the time we'd sailed the four miles to and then around Cabo Falso, Bud was freaked out because *Grendel* was only making three knots against the current. At this rate, we wouldn't have enough fuel to make it to Turtle Bay, which unnerved Mary. At four knots, she was certain we'd never make it to Turtle Bay or San Diego in time for her trip to Greece. So it began, the nightmare of Bud as delivery captain.

I had the 10 p.m. to 2 a.m. watch so I hit the sack early. The first few days were uneventful, with calm seas and *Grendel* making four knots against the current, and I was able to halfway talk Mary out of being afraid she'd miss the Greek trip. Her family was leaving on May 4 and I promised we'd arrive in San Diego well before then. No matter our speed, I'd make sure *Grendel* didn't run out of fuel in the middle of the ocean and go adrift. *How* I hadn't a clue. Under sail alone, we'd never make it in the three weeks before she planned to leave. Sailing without an engine required going hundreds of miles offshore, halfway to Hawaii, tacking away from the perpetual wind on our nose, then back, triangulated for San Diego, taking a minimum of twelve days. We might make it by May 1, three days before the Greek trip was scheduled to begin.

Bud sacked out after his 6 a.m. watch and I brought Mary morning coffee and breakfast, which I did every morning. We rehashed the fuel and timing problem, sticking close to shore, and avoiding as much adverse current as possible. Two days later, we were a hundred miles from Turtle Bay on what Bud said were the calmest seas he'd ever seen on nineteen deliveries from Cabo to San Diego. But we were only averaging four knots and needed to average five.

At noon, the ocean swells built with howling winds, and our speed dropped to three knots, making us miserable and Mary badly seasick for only the second time in the years we'd been sailing. The motion made for upchucking weather, and it was too dangerous to cook on the stove. Thus, we could fix no hot meals. The engine heat overpowered the refrigerator, which was unable to keep our provisions cold, so we repacked the food in plastic containers and put them in the always cool bilge.

The weather turned icy, forcing the three of us into polypropylenes and jackets. During the first twenty-four hours, Mary was able to eat only one banana, but her queasiness reduced her bitching over the fuel situation and the severe motion. When she rose from a stupor in the morning, she said she would never forgive me for making her help with this delivery. And the weather hadn't even gotten bad--yet.

An hour later, we were sitting in the cockpit when Bud remarked that we'd had the best seas conditions he'd ever had on a delivery. If Bud had seen the look Mary gave him, he would have shriveled up and died. Without the mainsail drawing well, we wouldn't have been making any headway against the swells and the ever-stronger current on our nose.

At 9 a.m., the engine died. We'd run out of fuel, which initially gave everyone heart failure, not knowing exactly how much fuel was left. We found only two containers remained, so we siphoned that into the tank and restarted the engine, and were back slogging against the unrelenting rollers that pushed us a foot back for every foot forward. We'd counted on making Turtle Bay in forty-eight hours, but hopes were fading. The GPS clocked four knots over the ground. The motion felt more like three knots to me.

Bud spent his watches reading Mary's complete Sherlock Holmes. He also stayed up for two or three hours on Mary's watches, telling her stories for hours, expounding on AA, diving, airplane mechanics, ex-wives, and children, along with theoretical girlfriends in Oregon and La Paz. Bud was good company for Mary but as a result, he got almost no sleep.

What a difference a day made. Twenty-four miserable hours later, the engine packed it in, permanently. Bud thought it'd thrown a bearing or rod because it wouldn't turn over. Since 5:30 p.m. the day before, we'd ignored an intermittent clunk from the engine, but after the last doozy of a clunk, except for the whisper of wind in the sails, we continued in complete silence.

We unfurled the 150-percent genoa, which pushed the rail below the water and doused everything on the deck above and in the cabin below, including us. Mary panicked and Bud gave us a tongue-lashing: To make substantial progress on a sailboat required putting up the largest sails, and that always resulted in a wet boat. But *Grendel* was taking on so much water we had to douse the genoa and put up the storm staysail and storm jib, which slowed us to two knots.

Mary was continually seasick during the next thirty-six hours of wet and mayhem, Bud was crotchety and frustrated, and I was worried that Mary would miss her plane to Greece and we'd be left adrift in the middle of nowhere. Everything in the cabin below was soaked with salt water: our clothes, bedding, audiotapes, and the two hundred books Mary needed since she read an average of one a day. Under full sail, water sluiced everywhere, and we had to pump the bilge, continuously.

The wind died after twelve hours under small staysail, storm jib, and single-reefed mainsail. In twenty-four hours we made only eleven miles toward Turtle Bay, which was still 110 miles away. A single glimmer of hope came yesterday afternoon when *Eliza* called us, asking if we had diesel available. We said no, but Mary insisted we needed a tow, which neither Bud nor I would ever ask for. We sailed up to *Eliza*, two miles away, and found a thirty-six-foot Columbia. They took us in tow with a five-eighths-inch three-strand line, but the tow reduced *Eliza*'s forward progress to two and a half knots. So, they cut us loose. We sat becalmed, over a hundred miles from the closest fuel.

In the morning we discussed running south, back to Cabo. Mary was for it big-time, but we had no wind and when the wind came up, it'd take at least three days to sail to Cabo. Mary spent time on the radio, calling every boat we heard: *Charlie Girl*, *Tall Cotton*, *Harmony*, and *Snowgoose*. None were close enough or willing to give us a tow. We tried drying a few clothes on deck but knew they wouldn't be wearable until washed in freshwater. Otherwise, the salt-impregnated cloth would irritate your skin and make it impossibly itchy.

We thought it'd cost five hundred dollars for a tow into Turtle Bay, which was all the cash we had, and I couldn't remember whether there was a bank or ATM to get additional funds. Bud made a show of working on the engine, saying, "Maybe we can get underway," but I knew he was only trying to make Mary feel better. We weren't eating enough, especially Bud, or drinking enough water. I always looked on the bright side, telling Mary we were still alive, healthy, and hadn't gotten polio, but she wasn't amused. We washed our hair in fresh water and felt better.

The wind went from zilch to twenty-five knots in half an hour, and we continued to sail north for three hours, tacking to clear Point Abreojos into Turtle Bay. After an hour of seawater sweeping the decks and funneling into the cabin below, Mary was in tears, accusing Bud and me of ruining everything she owned. So, we tacked and water flooded into the cabin from the other side of the boat. After two hours of drenching the cabin on the only two possible tacks, we'd only made two miles and still couldn't clear the point to turn into Turtle Bay.

Mary insisted we turn around and head back to Cabo. I agreed, and Bud sort of agreed, so at 6:45 p.m. we turned southeast. We'd given up after five days, three days motoring and two days sailing, and were still only halfway to San Diego. But it was good because Mary felt so much better.

We thought it'd take four days to reach Cabo. The first day we made over a hundred miles, but only eighty-five miles on the course because we couldn't sail directly toward Cabo without jibing. I had oatmeal with apples, sugar, and cinnamon for breakfast. Bud ate nothing and Mary was too seasick to eat. For dinner, Bud and I had potatoes and onions with a Milky Way candy bar for dessert. The boat was a wet mess, and we worried about losing the wind and having to sit becalmed for a week. In my opinion, the engine burned up because Bud ran it at excessive RPMs. I'd warned him about that every day, which made him turn red and breathe heavily, ultra-pissed off. Mary's only interest was taking a shower, the first one in six days.

The bunks were sopping wet and we had no way to dry them, which made sleeping miserable for Mary and me. Bud had stowed a dry sleeping bag in the only boat cupboard free of water and slept relatively well on the only settee that wasn't completely soaked. Mary read and sat and slept and complained, taking only a single watch from 10 p.m. to 2 a.m., when she was mostly supervised by Bud and regaled with his war stories.

With gale-force winds at our back, we made another hundred-mile day toward Cabo, surfing over heaving seas and swooping down rolling waves like a thoroughbred racehorse. We arrived at the Cabo marina at 3 a.m. on Monday, as projected, an hour after losing the wind a mile before the entrance, drifting toward rocks in the harbor. I launched the dinghy on rowdy seas and tried towing *Grendel*, but the surf was far too treacherous. So I tied the dinghy to Grendel's stern, and we used the outboard to motor into the marina, exhausted, wet, and cold, having had no sleep for twenty-four hours.

We first had to find a mechanic to determine whether the engine was worth repairing and, of course, ran up against the usual delays. After locating four mechanics and contacting the first one, we had breakfast ashore. Two mechanics agreed to survey the engine the next day at 8 a.m. and the other at 10.

After we paid Bud $150 for his assistance, he caught a bus to La Paz. Mary started with the first of seven laundry loads and split a whole roast chicken for lunch. Then we slept twenty-four hours straight, passed out on dry bedding slung across the dining table. The table made for an appallingly hard bed--tilted and narrow--but we slept well, uninterrupted the next morning by the arrival of a single mechanic.

I recontacted the two mechanics and one said he'd be there within the hour, and the other promised to show up at 1 p.m. Neither appeared. When again contacted, the first mechanic said he'd be there by 7:30 a.m. the next day and promised he could fix the engine for $600 plus parts, sight unseen. Right.

We surveyed the boat lockers and found the set of Harvard Classics was only damp, but our atlas was soaked. Our sodden clothing required another fourteen loads of laundry. After a marathon laundry day, I stowed my clean clothes while Mary packed hers for Phoenix.

The next day we rushed back from breakfast just in case the mechanic would show up as promised at 7:30. But he didn't and it wasn't a major surprise. I walked to the mechanic's garage and he'd taken another job but promised to come over in half an hour. He showed up at noon, listened to the engine, and agreed to pull it at 6 a.m. the next day. We counted it a miracle when he showed up at 6:30 a.m. with two helpers. It took four of us to pull the engine out of the bilge, onto the deck, into a cart, and onto the back of his pickup. He assured us his original estimate of $600 plus parts was accurate but said it'd take four to six weeks to repair, which was an appalling estimate. Marina fees would cost over $1,100 and we'd already spent $2,600 for parts to rebuild the engine.

This naturally stressed Mary out, making me angry and her angrier, compounding the strain. We argued whether to haul the boat and ship it overland to San Diego, which would cost three to four thousand dollars, but would save marina fees, months of delays, and potential problems with U.S. customs. I thought Mary would be ecstatic to escape Cabo for Greece in a week, but she said she almost canceled the Greek trip to stick around and help fix *Grendel*. Right. I wouldn't stick around if offered a trip to Greece! April 30 marked one year to the day when I'd quit my cushy government job, and began my so-called circumnavigation.

13

May 1994

It took five days to dry out the boat, wash salt-laden clothing, and reposition two hundred wet books every few hours so they'd dry in salt air with a hundred percent humidity. Mary and I quarreled the last few days before she flew back to Phoenix, stressed from the cost of repairing the engine on a tight budget of $1,350 a month, all I had left after paying $650 in child support. Now we'd have to berth *Grendel* in an expensive marina for a month. Mary promised to meet me to watch the Suns/Warriors playoff game but didn't show up. She pled illness the next morning and after our resulting argument, she refused to speak to me for the first time since we'd known each other.

Mary mellowed, promising a super day before she flew to Phoenix for the Greek trip. We had breakfast and lunch out with party time all day long, though also managing to pack three boxes of books and three suitcases full of clothes for her trip. At 6 a.m., we carried her boxes and suitcases to the dinghy dock next to the airport shuttle. She called her mom twice to confirm her 12:30 p.m. arrival and caught the shuttle to the San Jose del Cabo Airport.

I called the Atomic 4 dealer in San Diego to price parts, and he said it'd cost $1,500 for the crankshaft alone. He'd throw in the bearings and gaskets for $1,400, though it'd cost another $600 to ship and assemble the parts. I called Mary to have her mail a check to the San Diego Atomic 4 dealer and for the third time began reading the *Deptford Trilogy*. Though I'd miss Mary, I was looking forward to the third Suns/Warriors playoff game and three quiet weeks alone.

Jerry, of Ensenada hooker fame, sent a fax from Tucson. He and his friend Dale were flying to Cabo for the long Memorial Day weekend, which would relieve the tedium of unending chores required to get *Grendel* ready to sail, though interrupting my hoped-for quiet time. I had to fix screens, reorganize empty storage, clean the boat inside and out, and watch the NBA playoffs, the last one the most important. Maybe I'd have *Grendel* organized and anchored out of the expensive marina by Memorial Day. Right.

It was depressing to sit around waiting for things to happen, relieved only by tedious chores. I didn't know how to repack the boat without knowing whether Mary would come back down to help with the next delivery attempted to San Diego. The only glorious thing was having time to write. I sent faxes to Bud, pleading for help with the next delivery.

The total cost of the engine parts was $1,675, a few hundred over my monthly budget, excluding the pricey marina with daily rates only and no monthly discount. I reported the numbers to Mary and tried to lighten the blow by insisting it was only money. She said she hoped I hadn't thrown up and sounded ecstatically happy to escape to Greece for a few weeks.

I relived nightmares of our last attempt to sail to San Diego, dreading the next one. Would a rebuilt engine make it? How crappy would the weather be? We'd be living with little sleep and lots of stress twenty-four hours a day for two weeks, longer if unlucky. I needed nine hours of sleep but only got two hours sailing up the Baja. My dream was to arrive in San Diego, sell the boat, and hope Mary recovered from the experience. The highlight of the day was the Suns/Warrior's, Game 3. I thought it was funny how I missed Mary, even though there'd been occasions when I couldn't wait for her to leave.

Getting back to daily writing was difficult. The writing felt pedantic compared to the reality of sailing catastrophes. I took a batch of books to the Broken Surfboard to trade, returning with Elmore Leonard and Ray Bradbury, whom I'd met at the Santa Barbara's Writer's Conference. I also got Grafton, Heinlein, Gardner, Parker, Updike, McDonald, and Francis.

Bud still hadn't said whether he'd help with the delivery, Jerry hadn't mentioned when he was arriving, and I hadn't heard from Mary, who was leaving for Greece the next day. But I felt great because the Suns swept the Warriors in the playoffs and would next play Houston. I tried to summon the energy to fix the winches, but walked to the bus station instead, checking on the fastest bus to La Paz, planning for when I'd have to fetch the new engine parts.

A week later, I found out the check for the parts had cleared, and the parts would be shipped to La Paz in a few days, reminding me of the unending delays in Mexico. Meanwhile, I stayed within my seventeen-dollar-a-day budget, excluding the marina slip fee, but missed Mary, rebuffing several nice-looking ladies at happy hour, and while watching NBA playoff games. I've always been borderline antisocial.

Brenda called me from *Liberty*, a forty-two-foot Choy Lee Clipper she shared with Richard, saying she was stopping by to see me. Before Mary moved on the boat, I'd corresponded with Brenda about joining me on the *Grendel*. She turned out to be friendly, taking my picture and promising to send me a copy as soon as she arrived in Costa Rico with Richard.

I still hadn't taken the winches apart for lubrication but had happily reached the last thirty pages of *The Deptford Trilogy*, which totaled 843 pages. The mail delivered long letters from three friends in the States, cheering me up. A touted solar eclipse was a bust, but I was able to wash the entire deck during its theoretical arrival. I got into a rut of daily happy hour hamburgers, fries, and drinks at Latitude 22, dirt cheap, watching the most playoff basketball ever.

I finally faxed Joe Samek at the San Diego Atomic 4 store, asking where the hell my engine parts were.

The Suns were the only good news. After being down twenty points in the fourth quarter of the first playoff game, they beat Houston in overtime. Rah, rah, rah. I got around to reconditioning the winches, which I'd over-greased three years before. It took all morning, but they were rendered as supple as a whirligig.

Brenda and Richard didn't quite make it to Costa Rico, stopping by to tell me they'd had to turn back when a diesel fuel injector seized up fifty miles offshore. We had drinks, toasting the innumerable joys of sailing, promising to reconvene for happy hour before they left again, knowing it might be weeks before parts and repairs coalesced in Mexico.

I missed Mary but wondered how well we'd get along when she returned. It was silly for her to drive to Cabo, only to turn around with a few books and clothes off the boat, though that would make room for my folding bike in the cabin below. I hoped to hang the dinghy off the stern instead of stowing it amidships, where it impeded sail changes.

After a week, Joe Samek faxed me back, saying the check had taken ten days to clear, and he'd ship the engine parts in a few days. I ground my teeth and wondered how long it'd take Mexican customs to clear the parts for delivery. Three weeks or three days, baksheesh essential.

Tom on *Bastante* called. They'd turned around before Costa Rico and sailed back to Nuevo Vallarta. They'd leave the boat there for the summer while working in the States to replenish their sailing kitty. Tom commanded big bucks as a journeyman carpenter. In the fall, they'd sail to Panama, and through the Canal to the Caribbean. He gave me their phone number in Phoenix and I promised to call when next in town.

While watching Phoenix/Houston Game 3, two guys from Houston wandered in and their eyes popped when they saw the game on. They had a good ole time because Houston shellacked the Suns.

Back at the boat, I started working through magazines, canceling subscriptions because they cost a fortune to forward in the mail, stopping *National Geographic*, *Writer's Digest*, *Cruising World*, *Ocean Navigator*, and *World Press Review*, the last one now unfortunately defunct for decades. I still missed Mary but realized if she were here, it'd be no rose garden. We were both incurably independent: hers perfected by impatience and mine by obstinacy.

Tillicum from Vancouver with two German shepherds onboard rented a slip near me. I felt completely antisocial and didn't even say hi. Richard on *Liberty* asked the net if anyone knew where to find a high-pressure diesel line, obviously having no luck finding parts the last few days. I saw Brenda and Richard fueling up but didn't bother to say hi. They called later but I had the radio off all afternoon.

I was frustrated by the perpetually delayed parts, knowing it was likely they wouldn't arrive for weeks, but the weather and living in Cabo were pleasant. I got by on my daily budget, including food, restaurants, bars, gin, laundry, and expensive coffees while writing on the waterfront at Francisco's next to the marina. Locals wandered in front of Francisco's hawking cheap silver jewelry to uninterested gringos, mainly women and couples down for a few days at the beginning of the low season, staying at the gorgeous resort hotels strung out east of downtown.

Cabo Isle Marina was big enough to berth two hundred boats on fifteen docks, filling the north half of Cabo's inner harbor. At 5 a.m. every morning, fishing boats roared to life on D Dock, startling everyone out of their wits, or at least me, but that got me up and going. I hadn't missed a day of running since Mary left.

Cabo weather suddenly became less pleasant, ninety-three Fahrenheit, and humid as hell yesterday, so I rigged the wind scoop to divert breezes into the cabin below. I was happy to be making progress on writing, up to page seventy-three in the first draft of *Scribes*. Ron, my mentor for the first book, *Myths of the Tribe*, was anxious to read *Scribes*, but it'd take years for me to draft, revise, and edit the manuscript before I could send it to him. I was sure he'd enjoy it because he, a Catholic brother, and I were the protagonists.

Besides the wind scoop, I hoisted a bimini to shade the cockpit, hosting Brenda and Richard for cocktails before dinner together at Ranchos. After cocktails, they showed me around *Liberty, Wowza*, a spacious forty-two-foot Choy Lee. They were kind enough to say good things about *Grendel* and I gave Richard a few magazines he liked. I saved the rest for Mary, along with *The Deptford Trilogy*. We drank a few too many beers at dinner and wandered around Cabo afterward. A spray painter created an exclusive painting for Brenda but she rejected it. She also sent her enchiladas back at dinner, saying they were too spicy. Brenda tossed down the beer and was nicely affectionate with Richard, holding hands most of the evening. They talked about running around nude on their boat, the same as most cruisers do. Mary and I seldom wore clothes aboard. After this evening, I concluded Brenda was a whiner, a spoiled American Princess, assuming that isn't too politically incorrect.

I suffered a sad day watching Houston trash the Suns at Latitude 22 over my usual Big Mike Burger. After writing all morning, I lunched on deck under the bimini and the wind piped up to thirty-five knots in the harbor. Twenty-five boats had taken shelter in the harbor, and the wind had stranded a dozen tourist boats inside the marina. I finally met nearby *Tillicum*, who was wearing a delectable bikini, and we later exchanged waves at Latitude 22. Whoop-de-do.

Copper Sky, a sixty-foot steel tourist dive boat, entered the marina in a thicket of activity. They'd lost a diver overboard the night before, and never found him. The story had been all over the net for two days. Disembarking passengers knew nothing about the disappearance, except they hadn't found the diver, and were amazed everyone onshore knew as much as they did, which wasn't much. *Copper Sky* was well known in Cabo because of a previous action, filing a $150,000 salvage claim against a boat it'd towed a few months before.

I whizzed along with writing, up to draft page eighty-four, aiming for 125 pages before editing and polishing. Rosalinda from *Tillicum* invited me to a potluck on B Dock that I'd already decided to skip but I promised to reconsider after a nap. Rich and Brenda showed up but I said come back later because I was so ready to take a nap. However, I invited them to the potluck and said I might see them there. Short and rude. Richard had fixed his fuel line, and they would head offshore the next day, and I resented still having no engine parts.

I bought supermarket peanut butter cookies for the potluck and was disappointed that Richard and Brenda weren't among the twenty-five cruisers attending. Maybe I shouldn't have been so rude. During the hour I stayed, I met several interesting characters: Jerry on *Dolphus*, who controlled the radio net and owned the Cabo jet ski franchise; a couple on *Triton del Mar* reminiscing about San Blas, though she preferred Z-Town; and Ed on The *Farm* on a Ranger 33. Ed was a tall, skinny character who'd constructed an extraordinarily high dodger for *The Farm*, saying, "Every farm needs a barn." Otherwise, the potluck was boring.

My budget allowed coffee at Francisco's two days a week. Today's coffee failed to salvage the day because the Suns lost the third

164

game to Houston, I hadn't heard a word on the whereabouts of the engine parts, and Mary wouldn't arrive in Phoenix until Monday. The high point of the day was seeing four Mexican cops with Uzis, boarding *Copper Sky* to investigate the missing man overboard. Calling their weapons Uzis was a gross guestimate since I know nothing about guns.

The next day was my fifty-first birthday, celebrated by cleaning the boat inside and out. *Tillicum, Liberty,* and *Claire Bryant* left for San Diego, and I stood envious while waving goodbye. An hour later, *Claire Bryant* reported twenty-five-knot winds around Cabo Falso.

Marco Polo, the superyacht that'd brought parts for *Grendel* to La Paz months before, docked in the marina with Bud aboard. Bud spotted me, insisting I was stupid for ordering parts by UPS because they'd take weeks to arrive. He said I should have taken the bus to San Diego and gotten the parts and I failed to mention that I simply didn't want to.

Ed on *The Farm* told me *Pilgrim* was driving to LA with a trailer and would return in four or five days, bringing back anything anyone needed. Too late for my parts. Not the best birthday I'd ever had. I missed Mary and felt completely antisocial, uninterested in dealing with anyone for any reason.

Bud also said no one would be available to help deliver *Grendel* to San Diego, mocking me for staying in the marina instead of anchoring out for free. He rightly suspected I was too lazy to dinghy into Cabo every day. Two Ham radio operators in La Paz called to say they were keeping a lookout for my parts and would let me know as soon as they arrived. Pete on *Holly Ann* also said he'd fax me as soon as the parts hit

165

La Paz. Instead of celebrating my birthday with copious alcohol, I considered splurging six dollars on a banana split at Baskins-Robbins but instead decided to wait to share one with Mary when she arrived.

My birthday dinner at Latitude 22 featured the usual special, Mike's burger, and fries, but I splurged with a margarita instead of a Coke or beer. I saw the *Copper Sky* skipper leave the marina, arm in arm with the four cops with Uzis, who escorted him past the restaurant's big picture window. The Suns topped the day off by losing to Houston by twenty-three points. I wasn't looking forward to the next game two days later, figuring it be the Suns' last.

When I stepped on the boat, Bud called on the radio, ranting about how it'd take a month or more to get the parts to La Paz by UPS. He said they had to be stuck in Mexico City customs, and I should have gone up to get them. The fact he was right didn't make my day. He said *Marco Polo* had ordered an autopilot part from New York and had it air-freighted to San Diego overnight. The first mate flew up and was back in Cabo the same day. Damn, but *Marco Polo*'s budget was a bit grander than mine.

Les on *Free Spirit* stopped by to tell me his schedule was full with boat deliveries to San Diego and he wouldn't be able to help with *Grendel*'s delivery. He was leaving tomorrow to take a catamaran up and had another delivery starting June 15. For the first time in seventeen days, I did one load of laundry, including towels. Clothing was optional for the antisocial in Cabo.

I headed to the Broken Surfboard to watch the Suns, certain Houston would eliminate them from the playoffs. But things started looking up with an excellent fresh fish combi and margarita, four dollars including tip. The Suns game started late and I blew ten dollars on beer celebrating until midnight, euphoric after the Suns won big. Game 7 day after tomorrow!

The San Diego marina was two hundred dollars a month less than the Cabo Marina, so I rationalized that Cabo wasn't expensive, but I could rationalize pretty much anything. Buying *Grendel* four years ago had been the happiest day of my life. My new happiest day would be when I sold *Grendel*.

The morning net announced that *Clair Buoyant*, which had left three days ago and was well known around the marina, had grounded on the beach twelve miles south of Magdalena Bay. Their worst sailing day ever. I'd forgotten the exact time of the Suns game, rushing to Latitude 22 where the game was starting. The Suns lost, which eliminated that distraction, unless of course, I stooped to watch the upcoming Houston versus whoever won the Utah/Denver series.

I borrowed a caulking gun to fix *Grendel*'s deck leaks from Ed on *The Farm*, hoping to keep our dozens of books from a re-soaking. At the Broken Surfboard for lunch, I was happy to meet Linda, a fortyish blonde lady with a Dutch boy haircut who hoped to crew on any boat headed to San Diego. I gave her my card and said we'd be heading up as soon as parts arrived. I thought another crew member would make Mary more confident with fewer night watches. I wrote an hour on *Scribes*, up to page one hundred, enjoying the solitude but missing Mary, knowing full well I'd miss the solitude when she returned. Jerry and Dale were arriving on Friday.

The morning net announced the Mexican Navy had rescued the couple on *Clair Buoyant* but no one knew whether the boat had been saved. A forty-five-foot powerboat abandoned ship after a transmission failure and was adrift south of Magdalena Bay, creating a hazard to navigation and a multi-$100,000 temptation for whoever might be able to salvage her.

I was proud of running and exercising for the nineteenth day in a row. I'd loaned the marina gate key to a couple on *Pepe II* who stopped by and invited me to breakfast, but I was busy caulking the deck. They returned in an hour and we went to the Broken Surfboard for *huevos rancheros* and coffee, discussing the exorbitant prices of the boats in the marina. *Paulina Dos* and 143-foot *Tamara* cost over five million, and just remodeling *Marco Polo* ran ten million, both with full-time Aussie skippers.

Bud was patiently waiting to help crew *Marco Polo* back to San Diego. On the way back to *Grendel* from the Broken Surfboard, I saw Bud and hoped he hadn't seen me. A block later, I wished I'd asked him to check on my UPS shipment because I knew he was going to La Paz. Mary was scheduled to arrive back from Greece at midnight. I looked forward to calling her tomorrow but knew she might stop in Florida for a few days, where her uncle owned condos.

The NBA playoffs justified a nightly party, attracting a raucous group for the Knicks/Bulls game, including a wild honeymooning couple. Few tourists could resist nightly happy hour specials at the Broken Surfboard, ample hamburger, fries, and a margarita for four dollars. I sat next to a group of four that spent over a hundred dollars on beer and shots, a week's allowance for me. A cruiser who'd turned back from the slog toward San Diego reported hurricane-force winds where *Clair Buoyant* had blown ashore. I didn't relish trying the passage again, but I didn't want to stay in Cabo a second longer than necessary.

UPS Tijuana left a message that before they'd ship the parts, they needed a copy of my passport ID and $228 for customs and taxes. I faxed back and said hurry up. Bud planned to leave on the delivery of *Marco Polo* today, but it was blowing a gale in the marina, heeling boats on their sides. Outside the marina in the harbor, winds were hurricane-force. When I stood up to grab a book, a gust hit *Grendel* and knocked me across the cabin, making me extremely happy I wasn't headed out. I helped rig a new furling jib for an arriving boat that'd blown out its 140 percent spinnaker while sailing down from La Paz, all the while eager to call Mary and see how her trip went, and whether she still loved me. Very anxious.

I tromped all over Cabo, trying to phone Mary three times. She finally answered on the fourth try. We had a great talk, arguing over who missed the other one more. Her uncle had crashed a moped on Rhodes with her on the back. She'd skinned her leg and butt, which was slow to heal, and making it difficult to sleep. She could neither drive nor sit comfortably. I gave her the sad rundown on the boat-parts saga, and how much they cost to deliver to Cabo. The next day, I called Mary to suggest she not fly down until her butt healed. No reason to come all that way just to take a few books and our bicycles back to Phoenix. *Grendel* wouldn't be ready for weeks, though I missed her and wished she were here.

Linda called to have breakfast at the Broken Surfboard and said she was committed to crewing. I'd keep looking for crew anyway because crewing plans fell through every day and you couldn't have too many backup crew.

Bill on *Sundown* lost his rudder and had to be towed into the marina last night. I was envious of Bill's seamanship because when he'd lost his rudder, he'd been able to jury-rig a replacement with a spinnaker pole. Seasoned cruisers, unlike me, were able to make do with anything handy. It'd taken him four days for what should have been a day and a half sail.

Bill was interested in crewing, so I introduced him to Ed on *The Farm*, who offered to help Bill sail back to La Paz. Then Bill would crew with Ed to San Diego, leaving the next day. Bill promised to call me from San Diego and if I still needed crew, he would fly down and help.

Jerry and Dale were due into Cabo the next day, but if the parts arrived in La Paz, I wouldn't be sticking around to greet them. I'd instead head to La Paz to pick up the long-delayed parts. I knew that when Jerry and Dale arrived, peace and tranquility would evaporate.

My primary accomplishment during three and a half weeks waiting for parts was twenty-four straight days of morning jogging and exercise. I tried to call Mary but her mother answered and wouldn't accept the charges. I got the feeling she didn't like me.

It was only a hundred yards from the marina to the Marina Fiesta Hotel, where Dale and Jerry had reservations, so I walked over to check but they hadn't arrived. Back at the marina, the parts had arrived, and I owed $283 for their delivery! I was tempted to call Bud, gloating that his prediction of months to deliver the parts was off by months. The parts weighed thirty-seven pounds. I lugged them to TJ, my Cabo boat mechanic at Dos Amigos Marine, appreciating every single pound, sweating in the Cabo humidity like a banshee. TJ said he'd have the repairs done in a day or two. Right.

I walked back, finding Jerry and Dale pounding on the marina gate, yelling at vacant *Grendel*. They'd brought a bag of mail and gifts from Mary, new Birkenstocks (this sailor's friend), and T-shirts from Istanbul and Thessaloniki. She also sent a mushy four-page letter saying how much she missed me. The mail also included a letter from ex-wife Joy, asking for more child support money. I already paid more than a third of my income in child support. From my viewpoint, two things were fortunate: the child would be eighteen in less than two years and blood was unavailable from a turnip. I gave Jerry and Dale a tour of *Grendel,* and Jerry sprang for expensive bowls of Marina Fiesta Hotel margaritas.

I hosted the morning net and received a call from Tom in PV. He'd found a safe place to leave *Bastante,* so Kay and Tom would be leaving for the States to make a ton of money over the summer.

As host of the net, I happily informed the cruising community that six Cabo cruisers had arrived safely in San Diego: *Ono, Bayonne, Time Bandit, Slipaway, Big O*, and *Mica*, coloring me envious.

I called Mary and ignoring the pace of Mexican mechanics, told her *Grendel* might be ready to leave in a week. We commiserated about her still sore butt, made worse by bronchitis. I then called Linda and gave her the same exaggerated estimate of how soon we'd be able to leave, and she told me a lady friend of hers might also be interested in crewing and would contact me to discuss.

That evening, Jerry, Dale, and I watched the last quarter of the Houston/Utah game at Latitude 22, along with an uninteresting hockey game. Mike, the owner, kept switching to hockey because Houston was stomping Utah. We yelled at him constantly to switch it back. Jerry wanted to visit the only topless bar in Cabo, a ritzy joint named Gitanos, featuring mirrored walls, black décor, and, according to Jerry, gorgeous women. By 10 p.m., the bar was packed and Jerry had already spent over a hundred dollars on three fifteen-dollar lap dances, innumerable dollars tucked front and center in G-strings, and a dozen margaritas for our little group. Dale left at 11, me at 11:30, and Jerry reported lasting until 12:30 when he staggered to Squid Roe, theoretically packed with promiscuous drunken ladies.

The next morning, I slept in, failing to run or exercise for the first time in almost a month. Jerry, Dale, and I convened for coffee at Francisco's where I introduced them to Ed on *The Farm*. Ed regaled Jerry about folks he'd known with Jerry's last name, but of course, none were related to Jerry, who was running out of cash, so I took him to the Banamex ATM and, as usual, it was out of order.

I made a list of projects that had to be completed before sailing to San Diego, from changing filters in the watermaker to rigging the bikes on deck and cleaning the bottom. I dreaded the trip, worrying about finding enough crew. Jerry and Dale were scheduled to fly out at 9 a.m. the next day, which would let me get back to preparations. I was still hoping to have the engine reinstalled by Tuesday.

Jerry insisted on one more night of partying, starting at Latitude 22, where the cruisers hosted a potluck every Sunday night. Since I brought nothing, I enjoyed the usual Big Mike burger, curly fries, and margarita, meeting a couple from Vancouver who was winding up four years of cruising Central America and the Caribbean. It'd cost them $38,000 to replace a mast lost because of a loose shroud, and four months to collect from Seven Seas Insurance before they could refit a new one. I was happy to find I'd sailed to more Caribbean islands than they had, all but Barbados and Dominica, though only on chartered boats that I didn't have to maintain, repair, find parts for, ship parts through customs, and other migraines. Dale begged off partying while Jerry and I spent an hour watching and chatting up women at Squid Roe and Latitude 22. I crashed, and Jerry continued at Gitanos.

I met Jerry and Dale for a last coffee at Francisco's. They came close to missing the 9 a.m. airport shuttle because Jerry, as usual, had taken hours to pack three enormous suitcases he considered necessary for three days in Cabo. To me, it'd felt like a week.

I got back to *Grendel* for most of the morning net and found Ed on *The Farm* had left to crew a delivery to PV. He left word for me to call him on the SSB if I needed anything. I walked to TJs, and he'd just started working on the engine, promising to get it done by Tuesday and installed on Wednesday. That'd leave one day to run and test the engine because TJ had scored tickets to an Eagles concert in Phoenix, a celebration of the band recently getting back together. TJ was leaving on Friday for vacation and the concert, creating a familiar sinking feeling.

Bud sent a nasty fax to me, which was easily summarized: If I could afford to stay in the Cabo marina for a month, I could afford to pay him twice as much to crew to San Diego. I didn't bother to respond or point out that staying in the marina was why I couldn't pay him more money. Thus Bud would not be crewing, but Mary called to report her butt was feeling better. She'd gotten a hundred-dollar ticket to Cabo and would help crew to San Diego. We wouldn't miss Bud.

14

JUNE 1994

Four days slipped away while TJ and Rodrigo assembled and installed the engine, which of course wasn't ready by Friday. They'd put it back together on Wednesday and installed it on Thursday, oiled by copious bottles of beer, but the engine wouldn't start because TJ had forgotten to install the filter assembly and accelerator, whatever they were. Now TJ was off to the Eagles concert in Phoenix. I paid him the six hundred dollars we'd agreed on after he promised Rodrigo would finish everything that needed to be done, which I hoped included an operable engine. The balky ATM at Banamex worked overtime for a change, dispensing one thousand dollars in two tries, despite normally restricting withdrawals to five hundred dollars a day, and seldom working.

Mary was concerned with Linda's sailing experience and wanted me to find more experienced crew. I wasn't having any luck doing that, though in my opinion, the more crew the merrier. I went to dinner with Bill and Ed, watching the game at Latitude 22, and we griped about the women in our lives. They persuaded me to join them at Gitanos but the experience was morose, and after an hour, I walked back to *Grendel*.

Rodrigo had gotten the engine started, so I spent the next day organizing fuel for the passage to San Diego. The first ten gallons contaminated the fuel tank, and the other forty gallons were also bad, so I returned them for a refund.

I walked over to Rodrigo's, letting him know the engine oil pressure wouldn't register over twenty psi though forty was normal. Also, the dipstick showed way too much oil. Rodrigo said they'd put in seven quarts and I screamed at him that the maximum capacity was only two and a half quarts. We siphoned out the excess oil and the pressure went up to forty-five. But how much damage had been done?

Linda dropped by after lunch, clearly worried about crewing. She asked about my mechanical skills and I candidly told her I had none, which unsurprisingly affected her attitude. Linda corralled a guy named Chavez, trying to convince him to accompany us. He seemed an honest and trustworthy guy, going with Linda and me to find fresh fuel. We filled auxiliary cans to lash on deck, along with thirty gallons for the primary tank, hoping to dilute the contamination.

Linda said either Bud or Chavez had to help crew or she wouldn't. I couldn't fault her logic and scheduled a breakfast meeting with Chavez the next morning, offering him two hundred dollars and a plane ticket back to Cabo. He promised to discuss the question with his wife.

With a quarter tank of bad fuel, the engine in gear wouldn't run over 1000 RPMs and I needed at least 1600. Bill was crewing for Ed on *The Farm*, which along with *Spirit of Freedom* and *Ship Aweigh,* was leaving for San Diego at midnight, and I was sorely envious. *Night Song,* with Roy and his wife, was still interviewing potential crew and I begged them to send me all extra candidates.

I got the engine restarted but still had low RPMs. Linda met me for an early breakfast and Chavez was a no-show. We walked to his house and talked to his sister, who said he wasn't interested in crewing.

I invited Roy on *Night Song* over for beers, and he suggested aligning the engine, offering to do it himself. He found defective distributor wires, which retarded the RPMs. With new replacement wires, the engine fired on all four cylinders, instead of just two.

I called Mary in Phoenix and told her I desperately needed her help with the delivery. She wasn't happy but found an inexpensive round-trip ticket for $135 and would fly back to Phoenix if she decided not to crew. It didn't help the situation that Mary was sick in bed with a fever. Linda said if we couldn't find more crew, she'd kidnap someone at random.

I doubled my offer to Chavez, up to four hundred dollars, and he didn't reject it outright. Roy, Linda, and I spent Saturday night at Baja Cantina, starting with happy hour. Linda left for a birthday party, so Roy and I retired to *Grendel* for serious drinking. The next morning, the engine refused to start, and then when it finally turned over, it ran ragged. I called Roy and when he came by, the engine flat-out refused to start. We went through all the engine systems, working until late afternoon, finding no compression in cylinders three and four.

Roy's wife Cole was due to arrive on the same flight as Mary, who showed up with a suitcase, backpack, and three boxes of books.

Cole somehow missed the flight. I bought dinner for Roy, Mary, and Linda at Latitude 22.

Mary and I made up and fell into bed, spending the next day trying to locate piston rings for the engine in Cabo or La Paz, naturally to no avail. We ordered rings from the States for $275 and spent the day trying to find someone to tote them down to Cabo. A chap named Lee had a friend named Jimmy in AA, who was driving to San Diego on Tuesday and back on Thursday. Lee thought Jimmy might bring our parts back if we asked nicely so we met them after their AA meeting. Jimmy was cool to our request, worried about failing to declare the parts to Mexican customs. But he finally said he'd do it if he could declare the parts and I paid the customs fee. That would add forty percent to the cost but would be less expensive than flying to San Diego, paying for a motel, and flying back. We told Jimmy to do it, settling the speedy delivery of the rings. I guessed Jimmy would skip the customs declaration and pocket the difference. No one I knew had ever declared parts to Mexican customs.

On the morning net, I asked whether anyone would consider towing us to San Diego. A fifty-foot steel boat named *Wherever*, powered by a hundred-horsepower diesel engine, offered a tow. Of course, we were interested, depending on the price.

Roy showed up with Cole the same time as *Ship Aweigh* returned to port, reporting that a vicious storm had beaten up *The Farm* and *Spirit of Freedom*, but by now they should almost be to Turtle Bay. Susan on *Pinniped* notified the San Diego net that we needed transportation to Cabo for our parts and chatted with Mary. Linda knew that if we got a tow that would cut her out of crewing and was cool to us after the morning net. Roy offered to pay her to crew on *Night Song* but this turned out to be impossible because Roy and Cole had a cat on board, and Linda hated cats.

Rodrigo inspected the engine and told us the rings were shot before they put the engine back together. They'd somehow forgotten to mention this minor detail.

Scott and Allyson from *Whatever* inspected *Grendel* and said a tow would cost three thousand dollars. We said no thanks, though the engine would be impossible to repair without re-boring the cylinders and installing larger pistons. We later found three thousand dollars would have been dirt cheap.

We were depressed after having spent over a thousand dollars in December on the engine rebuild. We'd either need a tow, or further iffy repairs in an unknown amount. At least I'd learned to never let an engine run out of oil, which I'd negligently done during other crises on the way down. All my fault. If I'd have let Mary buy a new diesel engine in December, we'd still be cruising.

We met Lenny, who owned a luxury boat in the slip opposite *Grendel*, but lived at El Pedregal. He gave us a ride back from the grocery store and a tour of ritzy El Pedregal. He also drove us by houses owned by friends of his, Barry Hilton, who owned Carl's Junior, Karen Carpenter, and the sprawling joint owned by the CEO of Paul Mitchell cosmetics. Lenny owned seven Taco Bell restaurants in LA and San Francisco and a meatpacking plant in LA. He was rich, bored out of his skull, and weirdly fascinated by us.

179

Roy, Rodrigo, and I pulled the engine and propped it in the cockpit, confirming it needed a valve job. Jimmy brought the new rings down in two days, and we were optimistic about leaving soon, celebrating over dinner with Roy and Cole. But the next day was a disaster. The piston rings were too large, the same problem that'd screwed up the last engine overhaul. Frustrated, we discussed the situation for two hours. She blamed me for all our problems and I pled *nolo contendre*, no contest.

Grendel's electrical system shorted out, shutting down the watermaker and the pumps for the bilge and sink. Roy and I spent ten hours during two days finding the cause and fixing it. Of course, Roy fixed it and I provided the beer. We ordered the proper-sized rings and paid $145 as a cash advance on a Visa card, including shipping to Hermosa Beach. We were flat broke.

The only respite was watching the playoffs between Houston and the Knicks. Walking to Latitude 22, we met Mike, who'd arrived from San Felipe after a two-month journey on a kayak named *Raven*. He was looking for a ride back to the States and would crew gratis for anyone who'd tote his kayak back. We suggested he talk to Roy on *Night Song* because *Grendel* didn't have the deck space to carry a kayak that large. Roy didn't have space either because it was a whopping, long kayak. Because Roy needed crew, he began helping Mike find a boat to carry the kayak back to San Diego.

A week later, *Grendel's* electrical system was still wonky, but we reinstalled the engine with new rings brought down by Jerry on *Dolphus*. I paid Roy for ten hours of work on the engine at his twelve-dollar hourly rate. We still had no electricity on the port side, which contained the only twelve-volt charging socket for the GPS. Roy spent three hours trying to fix it, but was unsuccessful and as a result, didn't charge me for his time.

We often tried to avoid Roy and Cole because they liked to hang around us a little too much, but we were always unsuccessful. Walking back from dinner, we chanced upon Jim Wood, an old friend from Phoenix who was the best friend of one of my best friends, both of whom had been on the Greek sailing trip. Jim was the same jolly guy but had slimmed down. He was staying in the hotel where Jerry and Dale stayed, paying $289 for a week's package, including airfare, but it was high season so Jim paid $589.

Bad news on the engine. The maximum forward RPMs clocked at 1100, worse than before the ring job. Rodrigo showed up to help with the engine, expecting to be paid in addition to the six hundred dollars I'd given to TJ. He and Roy drank us poor, going through three or four ballenas/quarts of Corona beer a day, each. After the compression test, Rodrigo went home and drank seven more ballenas, his excuse for not appearing until 10 a.m. the next day.

By 10 a.m. we had the engine going with low RPMs but still no fix for the electrical problem. The only answer, according to Roy and Rodrigo, was to re-time the engine. They decided that had to be the answer because they couldn't think of any other solution. Though I'd cleaned the greasy, horrible, oily cockpit, the mess we made naturally dismayed Mary. While we tinkered with the engine Mary spent the week on *Blossom*, the fancy powerboat owned by multimillionaire Lenny in

181

the slip across from *Grendel*. He'd invited us to use *Blossom* while he was off to Frisco for a week.

Roy and Cole showed up after I'd gone to bed early, but Mary kindly let me sleep, entertaining them for two hours. We planned to leave the marina after our "free" eight days a month. Another pipe dream interrupted by unexpected delays, such as helping *Pinniped* moor in the harbor, which took two hours.

Besides reading aboard *Blossom*, Mary whiled away time at Francisco's, or the Marina Fiesta Hotel with Colleen, whom I'd never met and Mary professed to despise. Rodrigo tried to read the Atomic 4 engine manual, but it was in English, so he was wasting his time. The amount of beer and pot consumed was disgusting because I'd paid for it. Roy smoked three bowls of our stash every day while a bowl normally lasted me for three days. I was a total lightweight, unable to function with more, using it mostly as a sleep aid. Bad influencers, these mechanics. But I had written most of the first draft of *Scribes* so all was well.

We'd been stuck in Cabo for two-and-a-half months, except for nine days trying to sail to San Diego when we broke the crankshaft and had to sail back to Cabo. We'd spent $2,400 for two sets of rings and crankshaft, plus five hundred for Roy, confirming a boat is a hole in the ocean into which you pour money. The engine ran, but a sea test proved a maximum speed of two and a half knots at full throttle, 1300 RPM without the alternator, 1100 with. We'd reached a dead end on the engine and now would be unable to motor sail to San Diego in the always severe headwinds. The only respite was watching Houston even the series with the Knicks at three-three. I had nothing to look forward to except two days off before the seventh game for the NBA championship.

With only six free days left at the marina, Roy and I sought advice from Art at Nielson and Beaumont marine in Cabo. We'd spent three thousand dollars on engine repairs, matched by the same amount last December. The new diesel Mary offered to buy would have cost less, about five thousand, including exhaust modifications. Then we discovered the latest disaster, water in the Atomic 4 pistons. The block had cracked and the head gasket was blown, making the engine worthless and bumming us out. But this discovery was almost a relief because it jolted us out of the hopeless cycle of trying to fix the damn engine along with the end of long working days for Roy. Art said our only solution was to buy an outboard big enough to push *Grendel* eight hundred miles to San Diego. So, we went shopping for a new outboard, hoping to sell it in San Diego two weeks later before the charges hit the credit card. This would cost far less than a tow. Optimists were us.

Rodrigo fabricated an outboard mount, and we found a new fifteen-horse Johnson outboard motor for $1,420, certain it'd sell for at least a thousand in San Diego. The new plan bucked up the spirits of the half dozen folks helping get *Grendel* ready to go: Kayak Mike, Roy, Cole, Rodrigo, Linda, and Mary.

We mounted the new outboard and had it going by late afternoon, planning to shove off on Saturday afternoon, our last free day at the marina. This schedule required dawn-to-sunset days of endless preparations: checking the rigging, buying, storing, and lashing down fuel cans, cleaning the filthy boat, road testing the outboard, and breaking it in after locating extra oil for the outboard, plus provisioning and a dozen other chores.

Roy suggested we remove the Atomic 4 propellor to reduce the drag, but when we dove the prop, we couldn't disengage it from the hull. Dragging a non-functioning prop would lop a knot off our speed, which might not sound like much but would mean traveling twenty percent slower and taking that much longer. Roy loaned us a generator because we had no alternator and needed to generate electricity to run the radar, watermaker, and refrigerator. We relaxed on our next-to-last evening, watching Houston win the 1994 NBA championship.

Mary was moody during our last few days in Cabo, unhappy that we needed Linda to crew. I felt bad about the situation but couldn't find anyone else to crew. Kayak Mike found a ride for his kayak and agreed to crew for Roy, who'd also run out of money. Mary was exhausted and didn't attend a farewell dinner at Linda's thirty-one-foot Airstream trailer for our friends. The trailer sat on a hill with a grand view over Cabo, where we watched the sunset over the ocean to the west and color spreading across the wide bay to the east. Linda had landscaped the property beautifully.

Our little group went back to *Grendel* and sat around reminiscing until 11 p.m., Mary saying how sorry she was to have missed the farewell dinner. Everyone left except Cole. Mary and I waited for Cole to leave, but she loved to yick-yack, failing to take the hint when Mary and I finally toddled off to bed. When we got up the next morning, we were relieved to find she'd finally gone.

The Cabo electric grid complicated last-minute chores, electricity going out from Cabo to La Paz. Our water tanks were only a third full, and without electricity to pump water, they couldn't be filled. Mary, Linda, and I took *Grendel* out of the marina and anchored near *Night Song* with Roy, Cole, and Mike aboard, ready to leave at midnight. Goodbye, Cabo, please!

We got off on schedule with *Night Song* right behind us, though they edged ahead at 4 a.m. Before rounding the cape on the crests of long waves, the outboard was difficult to keep immersed. It maxed out on RPMs, roaring when lifted almost clear of the water. After clearing the cape and turning north, we had almost no wind and calm seas for the first twelve hours. The smooth ride in gorgeous moonlight put everyone in a good mood.

Our luck lasted two days before the outboard gurgled to a halt, drowned from a dunking under saltwater. I was afraid we'd ruined it, panicked we'd have to spend weeks sailing to San Diego. For five hours we tried sailing with little wind, logging less than six nautical miles. I radioed Roy, and he said to pull the plugs, drain the carburetor, clear the water by pulling the starting cable, replace the plugs, and try starting her. This was exactly the precise sort of direction needed by a hopelessly non-mechanical captain. I finished the job at 3 a.m. and sent Mary and Linda to bed. I'd almost given up starting the outboard when it kicked over to shrieks of exultation. Mine.

We motored on a parallel course with *Night Song* seven miles away, pinpointed at 130 miles from Turtle Bay at noon. I worried about having enough fuel because the outboard sucked one and a half gallons an hour. The sea was the calmest we'd ever seen, pure blue and glassy with hundreds of dolphins stretching five miles along our course. Ten repeatedly swooped under the bow, clearly visible in shallow dives. The show lasted an hour, the most dolphins we'd ever seen. By dusk, we reached the entrance to Magdalena Bay, bobbing on a flat sea with hundreds of tiny lobsters, which lasted all night and into the morning. It took twenty-four hours to sail across the 120-mile entrance to Mag Bay. We stayed well off Punta Abreojos, where we'd turned around on our last try with Bud.

The wind kicked up to twenty knots with whitecaps, but the Johnson outboard hung in there, pushing ten-ton *Grendel* between four and five knots, depending on wave conditions. At night the seas became too rough for the outboard, and we switched to sail, still making four knots, but soaking wet on five hours of the close-hauled tack that was necessary to conserve fuel. We rounded Punta Abreojos into Turtle Bay, where I'd destroyed the radar on the way down. The weather calmed, and we spent a pleasant day motoring into the enormous bay, anchoring off the Turtle Bay settlement at 3 a.m., instantly falling into bed.

We rose at 9 and packed nine jerry cans in the dinghy, landing and heading down the dusty street, each of us carrying three or four cans. A chap named Hector stopped in a ramshackle pickup and offered to ferry us around. He took us to the fuel depot, lone bank, back and forth to the pier with water, fuel, ice, and provisions. We spent $300, most of that on fuel. *Night Song* arrived at noon, and Kayak Mike rode into town with us.

We finished at 2 p.m., forcing ten dollars on Hector for his first-rate help during half a dozen trips. Hector was smitten with Linda, calling her Novia (bride or girlfriend), at first refusing compensation. He asked us to meet him for dinner at 5 p.m. and we readily agreed. Hector arrived at *Grendel* freshly showered and perfumed, wearing fresh clothes, trying to impress Linda. But we were too tired to go to dinner, which crushed Hector. We invited him aboard for a beer but eventually had to shoo him away so we could take Mike back to *Night Song*. There Mary, Linda, and I had a happy attitude adjustment with Mike, Roy, and Cole. Dinner was pepitas, Cheetos, and popcorn, and we stowed the dingy on deck, ready to leave at 6 a.m. the next morning.

At 5 a.m., *Night Song* called. Roy was sick with the flu and had a temperature of 102. We took the day off to rest, waiting for Roy to feel better. I taped a tube to the outboard, so it'd run submerged. But I couldn't pull the heavy engine far enough out of the water to change the gear oil, recommended after ten hours by the manual and we already had ninety hours on the engine.

We were ready to leave the next morning at 4 a.m., which would let us clear Punta Eugenia and the bay by 6 p.m. to anchor at the north end of Big Cedros Island. Though Roy was still feeling sick, *Night Song* planned on being two hours behind us because the weather was good, and Roy wouldn't feel any worse under sail.

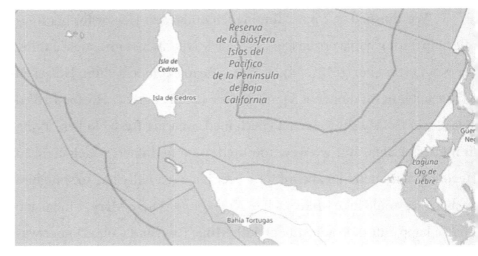

Turtle Bay and Cedros Island

We planned to arrive at San Quintin in three days to anchor and avoid the projected remnants of hurricane Carlotta, hoping that would give us southerlies to San Diego. Having the wind at our back would be a welcome change from fighting storms perpetually on the nose. *Night Song* left an hour behind us and dropped farther and farther behind.

The next four days were miserable. Mary and I argued whether to stop and wait for *Night Song* at our mutually planned anchorage off Little Cedros Island, which we reached at 3 p.m. I wanted to wait for Night Song, saying we were in it together, pointing out the constant help Roy had given us over many weeks. Mary wanted to continue full speed ahead, and Linda was politically neutral. Because Mary was so eager to keep going, I radioed *Night Song* and said we were continuing north and hoped Roy was feeling better. A severe storm began when we left Little Cedros Island, continuing without pause for four days.

The outboard engine drowned four times in huge storm swells. This meant removing the plugs and drying them out before we could get going again, an extremely precarious operation with *Grendel* rocking like a rollercoaster in terrible weather. We were deathly afraid of ruining the outboard and only being able to proceed under sail while trying to avoid the dangerous Sacramento reef, a graveyard for dozens of boats. As a result, we made little or no progress for four days, which added to Mary's budding hysteria. I was particularly worried about Mary missing the Greek trip. Linda was commendably stoic.

The next day we'd planned to cover a hundred miles but logged only twenty-five. Mary and Linda gave up, begging for a tow to San Diego. I asked Mary to wait until sunset when the wind normally dropped, and that's when the wind died in spades. We could neither sail nor make any northward progress. Without steerage, we might wash up on the reef, which made Mary anxious. She called for a tow on the radio and got a quote of seven thousand dollars. We were only 250 nautical miles from San Diego and could have gotten a tow from Cabo, eight hundred miles for three thousand dollars, highlighting our inability to gain hindsight before the fact. Mary and I agonized over spending seven thousand dollars she'd have to borrow from her dad, which he didn't yet know about. At an hourly rate, the tow would cost $175, totaling more than Mary's annual budget and over half of mine.

By noon on the fourth day, Mary insisted on a tow to San Diego. She confessed to being a wuss but was dog-tired of continuing crises with *Grendel*. Linda was also exhausted and had been seasick for four days, the same as Mary. I'd only been seasick once in my life, hungover from a party flight to Fort Lauderdale in the mid-1980s where we picked up a charter boat to the Bahamas early the next morning. Anyone seasick knows it's a nauseous and debilitating malaise, remedied only by acclimatization over time or simply stepping ashore.

The last straw was the Tillermaster. It quit overnight, which meant we'd have to hand steer for days and nights on end with little or no sleep, and we were already exhausted. The die was cast, and we ordered the gold-plated tow. *Tuna*, a steel cruiser with huge twin diesel engines, would handle the tow but wouldn't arrive for twenty hours, estimated time of arrival 8 a.m. the next morning. This gave us unending hours to fret over money dumped in the watery hole called a boat.

We washed our faces, pits, and hair for the first time in days, reading and relaxing, though the more I lay down, the more tired I became. It was exhilarating to begin phase two after the dissolution of my sailing dream, to sell *Grendel* and explore the world in some other fashion. But we'd suffered a financial disaster and would be on the cusp of bankruptcy for an unknown period of time.

We drifted toward the reef, all night long waiting breathlessly for the tow to arrive, scarcely able to keep from grounding in the light wind. The batteries were almost down to zero, which would have killed the GPS and radar, but after an hour of trying, we were able to start the generator and begin recharging the batteries.

The Coast Guard and *Timothy* radioed us, asking whether we were in danger. They were certain we'd lost our rudder or steering, asking incredulously whether *Grendel* was a sailing vessel. Mary again agonized over her impulse decision to spend over a year's income to save a few days of sailing.

Night Song radioed that she was leaving Cedros on calm seas and was headed our way. Then *Tuna,* the towboat, called asking whether we'd lost our rudder. With the light winds, we could have headed to Isla Geronimo and Punta Baja, arriving the next day and gunk-holing up the coast, taking about a week to get to San Diego. Assuming we could fix the outboard.

Mary felt slightly better when I pointed out with our skills and luck the estimated week could turn into several weeks. Still, Mary was going crazy, feeling she'd wasted seven thousand dollars she didn't have. We speculated about getting jobs in San Diego, though I couldn't think of what job I'd be able to get. My singular skill would require passing the California Bar, and it'd take six months just to prep for the exam.

Tuna arrived, creating unbridled jubilation aboard *Grendel*. One of their men swam over in a wetsuit, came aboard, and gave us a contract to sign.

Tuna's three-man crew ran around like cowboys, whooping and shouting as they set tow-lines. It took almost three hours to secure the tow in high seas, during which I rewrote *Tuna*'s contract. The first attempt to take slack off the towline broke *Grendel*'s bow roller, but *Tuna* made no more mistakes. A chap named Kurt swam over in a wet suit to retrieve the contract and we waited breathlessly, worried they'd read the changes and refuse the tow, but not a peep. We had such mixed feelings, wholehearted relief at soon getting to San Diego after three months trying, but oh, the money spent.

Tuna was in a tremendous rush, revving up to seven knots in heavy seas that pounded *Grendel* with massive rollers, sending water pouring everywhere, into the cabin, and sweeping the deck. As a result, I twice had to order *Tuna* to slow down. Then I had to stop the tow three times to re-secure gas cans on deck and retrieve the Johnson outboard, which came unmoored, trailing behind us like an albatross and giving me heart failure.

Every square inch of the boat was sopping wet from green water crashing over us for fourteen hours straight, soaking settees, bunks, equipment, clothing, and books. By 9 p.m. the seas died down fractionally, and I was able to stabilize the extreme motion with a reefed mainsail. We couldn't nap below, which had been swept with curtains of water, drenching the boat and us in unending cascades, burning our eyes with saltwater and soaking everything else. To keep from sinking, we had to pump the bilge every four to ten minutes all night long. No one slept.

Come morning, the seas calmed, and we were mesmerized by the extraordinary wake plowed by *Grendel*, one that only a super towboat could induce. We were traveling eight knots, far above hull speed, and I worried the deck cleats securing the tow would rip out and sink us. At dawn, we were off the deserted island of Colnett where I'd hiked for two hours on the way down, and where ocean swells had destroyed my spade anchor. Meanwhile, we were expected to arrive in San Diego between 8 and 10 p.m. Everyone was excited to step on solid ground, find a hotel, and take a shower, though we worried about clearing U.S. Customs. You never know what that bunch will get up to.

We arrived at 10:30 p.m. on July 9, 1994, dropped off by *Tuna* outside the harbor and towed in by Don on *Responder*, who owned Westow Company and *Tuna*. Don told Mary he'd incurred another five hundred dollars in expenses and wanted $7,500, and Mary agreed without a quibble, contract be damned. Her relief was profound at finally arriving in San Diego.

Don waited for us to clear customs, accomplished by 11:30 with no hassles, except a twenty-five-dollar fee. Don towed us to the Shelter Island boatyard, comping a slip for *Grendel* through Sunday, three and a half days out of his $7,500 fee. We paid Don with my credit card, which Mary later reimbursed because we've always kept our finances separate. We checked in at the Vagabond Motel, fifty dollars for two queen-sized beds, then to a midnight breakfast at Denny's, spending eighteen dollars. This left us thirteen dollars to our names. We showered and then crashed at two a.m. So happy to be in San Diego.

Excluding trips to Arizona, we spent the next four months at the Bay Club Marina, next to Humphrey's on Shelter Island. We listed the boat with a broker and sold all the equipment separately at swap meets for sailors, based on the broker's advice that buyers prefer to select their own added components. That meant uninstalling everything from the radar to the watermaker, and anything else we could pry off the boat.

The Bay Club was in a great location because Humphreys Restaurant next door hosted nightly concerts visible from *Grendel*'s deck. Without suffering a cover charge we watched, among others, the Neville Brothers, Smokey Robinson, Art Garfunkel, and Al Jarreau. Humphreys also offered daily happy hours with fancy hors d'oeuvre and inexpensive drinks that we and our fellow sailors took copious advantage of.

The Bay Club marina was a deal at three hundred dollars a month, with one catch: tenants couldn't live-aboard, but only spend weekends aboard. We got caught in September and were asked to pony up another $170 a month but spent half of September in Phoenix, which threw them off the scent. We skated until the boat sold in November.

Mary's dad loaned us a utility truck, the transportation we needed to take boat equipment to swap meets. The truck had its problems, most of which were fixed by Mary's dad on trips back to Phoenix. On August 31, the Bay Club towed the truck out of the parking garage because it'd sprung a gasoline leak. When we paid the eight-five dollar combination ransom and towing fee, the tow truck driver kindly fixed the leak in the truck's fuel line and only charged ten dollars.

Our time in San Diego was great fun, though we had lots of work to do. Impressing potential buyers of a boat without an engine required sanding and varnishing the teak, which was a four-day job, and cleaning every surface, which took months. Tempted by twenty-nine-dollar Southwest airline tickets, seven sets of friends came to visit, including Jerry, Morgan, and Marty. We spent time with a dozen cruising couples we'd met in Mexico, from Susan and John on *Pinniped* to Kay and Tom on *Bastante*. Roy and Cole on *Night Song* were constant visitors and showed us around Ocean Beach, where Roy knew everyone in his role as the local pot dealer.

The funniest episode occurred when we sold the watermaker to a potential buyer named Don. Mary held him spellbound and Don politely

194

asked if she would let him take a peek at her breasts. We laughed him off, finding it amusing, but Don showed up a week later with his wife, Judy, uninvited. We asked Don in front of Judy how much Don would pay as previously requested to see Mary's bare boobs and Judy dragged him away by one ear. Don had the balls to return a week later, again with his wife, but we ignored them both. And hurrah, I finished the first draft of *Scribes*.

Grendel sold after agonizing months back and forth with potential buyers, made difficult by the lack of an engine. We received an offer of $12,500 in late October and countered for $14,000, on tenterhooks because we didn't know where we'd end up next. RVing was our future, but after checking out a San Diego RV show, we realized we couldn't afford a new class B campervan, which cost $50,000 new. By 2021 they cost more like $100,000. But there were plenty of inexpensive used class A and class C RVs.

If we didn't sell the boat before the end of the year, we'd buy a used RV and head to Mexico. Otherwise, we'd find an RV in Europe and spend years seeing every country there. We'd found a book at the Upstart Crow Bookstore in San Diego's Seaport Village that described the ins and outs of RVing Europe, written by a couple who'd done exactly that for fourteen months. That hooked us, though we guessed it'd take us three years to see every country in Europe.

Buying an RV in the UK was out of the question because the pound was up to $1.55. If *Grendel* sold by November, we'd fly to Frankfurt, where the authors of the Europe RVing book had bought their

RV. We told our plan to everyone who'd listen, covering up our failure to sail around the world by instead RVing the world.

The negotiations to sell *Grendel*, all the equipment, and a final sea trial took until early November, and that was when the America's Cup competition began in San Diego, kindling a fire in the cruising community. We tried to hold out for $14,000 as *Grendel*'s minimum sales price because after deducting the broker's two thousand dollar commission, that'd barely give us enough to buy a decent used RV in Europe. But we had to drop the price by five hundred dollars because we'd left the dinghy on the list of equipment that went with the boat, though we'd sold it a month before. We were sweating bullets on closing the deal because November 17 was the last day to pay for the plane tickets we'd reserved for Europe.

We signed the sales papers for *Grendel* on November 7, 1994, the happiest day of my life. This sealed our European scenario. It took us almost three years to see all of Europe excluding Switzerland because we were too cheap to buy a Swiss travel permit. But we drove most roads in every other country, and took a car ferry from Athens to Haifa, Israel, tacking on Jordan and Egypt besides spending a winter in Morocco. The proceeds from *Grendel*'s sale, plus the equipment sold separately-- SSB, GPS, radar, watermaker, outboard motors, and other miscellanies-- totaled $18,600, about a fourth of the amount we'd invested in *Grendel* over the years. We were raring to leave, preparing by buying a book entitled *Nude Beaches of Europe*.

The Johnson fifteen-horse outboard had been on consignment for $1,400, based on new ones selling for $1,700 in San Diego. We'd paid

$1,420 in Cabo, and netted $1,200, not bad considering how many times it'd been dunked in seawater, ignoring the shockingly expensive tow.

On December 9, we flew to Frankfurt, Germany, with fifteen checked boxes and two folding bicycles, paying nine hundred dollars for the extra freight. Before the end of December, we were off RVing Europe. The airline failed to load our boxes and bicycles on our flight, so after waiting an hour for our luggage, we filed a claim with Continental Airlines. It took a week for the airline to find our boxes, which we retrieved from Nissan Freight in horrific traffic in a Frankfurt suburb. However, the airline lost the bicycles for over a month, finally authorizing us to buy new bikes when we were happily ensconced in the south of Spain. We were dashed the next day when Continental located our lost bikes because we'd already shopped for and fantasized about buying new ones.

RVing was a lot easier way to see the world. At least for us. We didn't have to worry about electrical and mechanical problems, severe weather, and sticky-fingered, turtle-slow customs. Mechanics were always within shouting distance in Europe, rendering my spectacular mechanical and electrical deficiencies irrelevant. We also easily found needed repairs in Asia, Africa, South America, Australia, and New Zealand, RVing full-time for two decades. I'd learned at least one lesson from our sailing adventure and never burned up another engine.

THE END

If you liked this book, please leave a review.

For our three years in Europe, see *RV the World*. Here's the first chapter.

RV the World

IN THE BEGINNING

THE MONKEY ON MY BACK: TO SEE IT ALL

For my part, I travel not to go anywhere, but to go. I travel for travel's sake. The great affair is to move; to feel the needs and hitches of our life more nearly; to come down off this feather-bed of civilization, and find the globe granite underfoot and strewn with cutting flints.

Robert Louis Stevenson

My earliest vivid memory is of a photo from an old geography book: Vesuvius in full-color eruption spewing fluorescent orange magma, torching rich Romans in Pompeii. This hit me between the eyes. *Whoa.* I really had to see that in person. What six-year-old wouldn't?

I could never kick this early memory, which evolved into a dream of seeing the world, the whole lot of it. My earliest ambition was finding the world's most fabulous volcanoes, my curiosity spurred by schoolteacher parents with a passion for travel and geography. I inherited a travel addiction, doomed to see the entire world or die trying.

I nagged my long-suffering parents to drive down every road, reasoning that we might stumble across Vesuvius anywhere. Humoring me, they drove down lots of dirt roads, many ending on the edges of deep canyons in Colorado, New Mexico, Utah, and Arizona, the Four Corners area where I grew up. They'd brought it on themselves, infecting me with a travel-and-geography obsession, insisting in return for my see-the-end-of-every-road harassment that I learn context, all the states, their capitals, and the capital of every country on the planet. I was crushed to find Vesuvius nowhere near the Four Corners.

An outlet for itchy feet fortuitously appeared when I was teaching at the local law school. A student said, "Hey, come help me try out my new sailboat." That day one of Arizona's many lakes became a scene of high comedy. By 10 a.m. we finally got the pole up. I later learned it was called a mast. Though we scooted down the lake in half an hour, downwind, it took until sunset to sail back as we cursed Gods whose proper names we didn't know—the Gods of tacking, coming about, and shifting winds. I was indelibly hooked.

After a few months of torture on my friend's Hobie Cat, including six crazy days sailing down the Mexican coast from Puerto Penasco to Bahia Kino, I finally enrolled—along with my wife, Mary—in a learn-to-sail course at the Annapolis Sailing School in San Diego. Then I tackled the advanced sailing course, which theoretically qualified me to bareboat charter.

Suddenly I wanted to sail around the world. People said, "But you live in Arizona. There's no water, except a few ridiculous lakes." By then everyone knew I'd gone stark raving mad—including Mary, but she

199

gradually contracted the insatiable wanderlust encouraged by my parents.

I captained seventeen charters in Greece, Turkey, Vancouver, Belize, and most of the Bahamas and Caribbean Islands. It was my responsibility to find a proper sailing vessel (best price), set up the charter, organize disorganized friends during bouts of personal disorganization, and then, once we arrived at the destination, find water, fuel, and a likely place to moor or anchor each night. I halfway learned to sail a dozen different sailboats while my accompanying friends coughed up three hundred dollars per person for the pleasure of crewing. Aren't friends fabulous?

The second most glorious day of my life was buying a dreamboat to sail around the world. I named her *Grendel*. Mary and I spent years flying on weekends from Phoenix to San Diego, putting every toy aboard, from mast steps to radar to a water maker. The big day arrived when, after saving every penny on a ten-year plan that stretched to eleven years, I sold everything and sailed *Grendel* out of San Diego Harbor.

It became abundantly clear that Dave and Mary sailing around the world was not exactly as it appeared in *Romancing the Stone* when Michael Douglas and Kathleen Turner sailed into the sunset. No, life on *Grendel* was more about *la problema del dia,* the problem of the day, especially for someone who'd flunked grade school shop and was the least mechanically minded in the history of the Montezuma County public school system in Cortez, Colorado. To sail around the world you not only need to know how to sail but also how to fix stuff—all the stuff, including mechanical and electrical— and you need the baksheesh to coax replacement parts through foreign customs.

Hollywood had done me a disservice—or perhaps, like those guys who count landing at an international airport as visiting a country, I was a dope. After a year we were still in Mexico, though far down the Pacific Coast. The Marquesas and Tuamotus islands were next on our itinerary, and as the specter of a thirty- to forty-day ocean crossing loomed closer, I faced up to my terminal ineptness with a multi-meter and a monkey wrench, and Mary admitted to hating unending oceans. A compulsive jogger, she found the deck was too small for laps. We turned north to San Diego, where I experienced my most glorious day, selling *Grendel*.

By no means was this the end of my dream of seeing the world but instead the true beginning. Living on a sailboat relegated us, two non-beach persons, to the coast, though 90 percent of what there is to see is inland. We found sailing the very best way to spend time fixing stuff in exotic ports, leaving little time for exploration.

We began international RVing in 1994. That year we flew to Germany and bought an RV with the proceeds from *Grendel*. We lived the next three years in forty countries, spending summers in the United Kingdom, Ireland, Norway, and Scandinavia and winters in Spain, Portugal, Morocco, Italy (where I finally saw Vesuvius not erupting), Greece, Turkey, Israel, Jordan, and Egypt, plus all the countries in between. Seventeen years later, though we have stopped full-time RVing, we're still RVing the world six months a year.

We've visited hundreds of scenic spots available overnight only by tent or RV. Among our favorite experiences have been overnighting within or next to:

- The Horns of Hittite, where the Crusaders met their final demise above Lake Kinneret (aka the Sea of Galilee), where we were visited by a helicopter.

- New Zealand's Mount Cook, framed by our RV's panoramic windows, and Milford Sound, which we had all to ourselves after the tour buses had gone home for the night.

- A remote beach in New South Wales, where we were surrounded by kangaroos.

- The world's most incredible ruins at ancient Petra, and definitely by ourselves in remote Wadi Rum, where Larry of Arabia hung out, both in Jordan.

- Alice Springs in Australia's Northern Territory, where we watched a full eclipse of the moon atop our RV.

- The wind-hewn canyons of the Negev Desert. A French canal and an ancient French monastery in a primeval forest.

- Hobart Bay and Cradle Mountain in Tasmania. Purnululu National Park in the orange-and-black-striped mountains of the Bungle Bungles, and at the confluence of sandstone slot canyons in Karajini National Park, in Western Australia.

- The waterfront in Ushuaia, Argentina, the southernmost city in the world, where we watched ships leave for Antarctica, and in

Tierra Del Fuego National Park, outside Ushuaia, at the foot of the last of the Andes, on the Beagle Channel.

- Vesuvius overlooking the bay and the lights of Naples.
- The canals of Bruges, Amsterdam, and Venice. (Unfortunately, the Chinese government prohibits driving an RV to the canals of Suzhou).
- Finland's many lakes, surrounded by reindeer. The waterfront in Stockholm, where we camped for a week.
- Lake Titicaca in Bolivia. Another Bolivian favorite is Mount Sajama (21,000 feet), where we camped at 15,000 feet next to hot springs a few kilometers from the border with Chile on a lake perfectly reflecting twin Fuji-esque cones.

The week before I quit playing lawyer, several friends said they envied my plan. The brevity of life had been vividly illustrated to them. They, like me, had always treated life as if it went on forever. One guy's brother had been diagnosed with inoperable cancer, a month before his scheduled retirement. Another's father had prostate cancer, chose the operation, and died two weeks after retiring. Mary's boss had dreamed of buying an oceangoing fishing boat but kept putting it off. He needed to add to his retirement kitty. Just before we left he was diagnosed with a brain tumor and died a year later. Do it now, whatever it is you want to do. If we don't do it now, the odds are we never will. Perhaps along the way, you'll find the world's most picturesque volcano.

Made in the USA
Monee, IL
20 May 2022

96787585R00115